D1495225

SIGN LANGUAGE INTERPRETING

SIGN LANGUAGE INTERPRETING

Deconstructing the Myth of Neutrality

MELANIE METZGER

Gallaudet University Press   Washington, D.C.

Gallaudet University Press

Washington, DC 20002

Library of Congress Cataloging-in-Publication Data

Metzger, Melanie.
    Sign language interpreting : deconstructing the myth of neutrality
/ Melanie Metzger.
        p. cm.
    Includes bibliographical references and index.
    ISBN 1-56368-074-2 (hc. : alk. paper)
    1. Interpreters for the deaf—United States—Psychology.
2. American Sign Language—Translating.   3. Translating and
interpreting—United States—Psychological aspects.   4. Deaf—Means
of communication—United States.   I. Title.
HV2042.M37   1999   98-49308
419—dc21   CIP

To my parents
Jill and Eric

who taught me that I can

To Earl

whose longtime interest in this topic
and whose incredible focus
helped make this work a reality

Contents

Acknowledgments

MANY PEOPLE have contributed to this work. While it is impossible to adequately acknowledge each one, I am truly grateful to all of them. Special thanks are in order for Dr. Heidi Hamilton, whose confidence and guidance have been invaluable. Her very human application of linguistics to real-world problems has been inspirational. Dr. Ceil Lucas has also been a great source of inspiration, providing a model of scholarship that brings linguistics to the analysis of Deaf and hearing community interaction. I am grateful for her support and her contribution to this research.

Thanks are also due to Dr. Roger Shuy and Dr. Deborah Schiffrin for providing critical support as well as insight into the research process and product. Although I am ultimately responsible for the final product, these individuals have impacted the development of this work. I am truly indebted to them.

I am also indebted to all of those who took time out of their busy schedules to read and/or to discuss pertinent issues concerning this work or the related pilot study. Thanks to Byron Bridges, Nancylynn Ward Bridges, Dr. Valerie Dively, Earl Fleetwood, Beverly Hollrah, Dr. Robert E. Johnson, Dr. Scott Liddell, Keller Magenau, Dr. Susan Mather, Galey Modan, Dr. Carol Patrie, Dr. Elif Rosenfeld, Dr. Cynthia Roy, Dr. Deborah Tannen, Dr. Clayton Valli, and Dr. Elizabeth Winston. I would also like to acknowledge the students in my interactive interpreting courses at Gallaudet University who willingly shared their insights, intuitions, and questions about interpreting.

To all those who willingly participated in the data collection for this study, and to all those native language users and interpreters who shared their perspectives during the analysis of the data, I also am indebted.

Additionally, I would like to thank Ivey Pittle Wallace and Jenelle Walthour of Gallaudet University Press for their patience and hard work in bringing the manuscript to press.

Finally, I extend my heartfelt appreciation to my family and friends, who showed patience when I disappeared for months on end. I also express my gratitude to Jill and Eric, who read countless drafts and shared their unique perspectives on them, and to Earl, who never tires of theoretical discussions about interpreting issues.

1

Neutrality in Translation and Interpretation

IN DISCUSSIONS of the issue of interpreter neutrality, the anecdotes that interpreters and laypeople share suggest that the traditional perception of the interpreter's role as a neutral conduit of language is at odds with people's real-life experiences. For example, in an interpreted college course, a hearing student described how the class discussion was interrupted by the ASL-English interpreter, who said to the class, "One at a time please. I can't interpret all of you talking at once!" After a lengthy pause, the discussion slowly began again, with an attempt to limit the floor to one speaker at a time.

In another example, a hearing ASL-English interpreter described her exasperation while interpreting an incomprehensible speaker at a professional meeting. She finally admitted to the participants, "Just a minute, I can't understand what you're saying. And if I can't understand you, I'll bet half the people here don't understand you either. I'm sure you don't want to waste your time talking if you're not being understood . . . could you please say that again?"

In yet another account, a Deaf patient described the behavior of a hearing interpreter at a medical interview. The hearing doctor had just completed an examination and was encouraging the patient to make an appointment for surgery when the interpreter surreptitiously signed, "Don't make the appointment yet. Wait until I talk to you outside for a minute." The Deaf patient told the doctor he would take some time to consider the surgery, then met with the interpreter outside. The interpreter informed the man that there was

1

something about the way the doctor was talking that made the interpreter distrustful, and suggested that the patient get a second opinion. The Deaf man did so, and discovered that he did not, in fact, need the surgery in question.

In each of these stories, the interpreter makes contributions to the discourse that extend beyond mere renditions of other participants' utterances. The interpreters' alleged comments represent attempts to regulate interactions, to change speaker's discourse styles, and to judge people, in part, based on how they speak. More subtly, they represent apparent difficulties faced by the interpreters in attempting to provide access to real-life interactive discourse in which speakers frequently overlap (Tannen 1984), might intentionally speak in ambiguous ways (Kochman 1986), and whose linguistic strategies reveal subtle cues that are identifiable on the basis of cultural information not consciously considered by a native user of the language (Gumperz 1982). Yet, if interpreters really do confront such difficulties and subsequently initiate such contributions to interactive discourse, what is the actual rather than intended interactive relationship between the interpreter (and his or her utterances) and the participants relying on his or her services?

While this question clearly has ramifications regarding an interpreter's relative partiality in an interpreted encounter, it is important to remember that the aforementioned stories are merely anecdotal illustrations of the fact that interpreters contribute in a variety of ways to interactive discourse. As Gile (1990) points out, after many years of theorizing about interpretation on the basis of informal observation, it is necessary to pursue empirical studies of interpretation in order to engage in "a serious discussion of basic issues" (38).

For thousands of years, controversy has centered around the ways in which translators and interpreters can render source messages into target messages in as neutral a manner as possible. Some have argued that literal translations are truer to the original, while others suggest that free translations provide more appropriate renditions. However, until relatively recently, few have examined the utterances of interpreters in order to examine interpreters' contributions to the discourse of interpreted encounters. Recent sociolinguistic analyses of interpreted interactions indicate that the role of interpreters is not as neutral as much of the literature has either assumed or prescribed. In a recent examination of interactive interpreting, Wadensjö raises an important question with regard to interpreter neutrality: "Given that neutrality is a notion concerning relations, the question concerning dialogue interpreters' activities must be: neutral in relation to whom and/or what?" (1992, 268).

Wadensjö suggests that the interpreter must be neutral with regard to the participants for whom she is providing a service. While interpreters might feel more or less loyal to one or another participant, or to one or another of the participant's goals, the interpreter must keep these feelings separate from her task as an interpreter in order to successfully accomplish it. Wadensjö found that this need to maintain a distance from other participants actually contributed to interpreters' omissions of certain kinds of utterances. For example, when a participant foregrounded the interpreting task through comments such as "Say what he says now," the interpreter did not always provide a rendition of these comments (268); that is, the interpreter did not interpret the comment that had been directed to the interpreter. This example seems to raise an additional issue with regard to Wadensjö's question of neutral relationships: interpreters have the option of remaining neutral in relation to their own utterances, be they renditions of others' discourse or not.

Translation and Interpretation

Both translation and interpretation deal with the rendering of a given text into another language. Frishberg (1990) distinguishes between the two on the basis of form. That is, *translation* refers to written texts, while *interpretation* refers to the "live and immediate transmission" (18) of discourse that is spoken or signed. Both activities share certain commonalities. Regardless of mode, all texts can be seen to be "evidence of a communicative transaction taking place within a social framework" (Hatim and Mason 1990, 2). Moreover, many of the questions that plague the one also plague the other. Thus, the two are born of a similar history. As Roy (1989a, 1993) points out, assumptions regarding translator neutrality are related to scholarly discussion of the processes involved in the task of transmitting text between languages. The issue of a translator's influence on a text and the question of how to maintain neutrality in translation can be seen as an underlying cause of the historical dilemma in translation studies: literal versus free translation.

Undoubtedly, questions regarding the quality and appropriateness of translations have been in existence as long as the practice of interpreting and translating texts. Although face-to-face interpreting no doubt preceded written translation (Cokely 1992), the development of writing systems first provided the means by which to assess a translator's work. Thus began an unending controversy regarding the qualities that define issues such as accuracy and equivalence in translations.

Literal Translation

Aristotle was among the first to address concerns regarding a translator's influence on the translation. He emphasized the importance of accuracy in interpreting texts (Wadensjö 1992, 12), and the pursuit of accuracy and equivalence has continued throughout history. For instance, in 1506, Desiderius Erasmus, Dutch humanist, philologist, and translator wrote: "I have scrupulously tried to produce a literal translation, forcing myself to keep the shape of the Greek poems, and also their style, as much as possible. My goal has been to transcribe verse for verse, almost word for word, and I have tried very hard to render the power and weight of the phrase intelligible to Latin ears with the greatest fidelity" (from Lefevre 1992, 60). This emphasis on literal translation seems to deemphasize the role of the translator as an "interpreter" of the original text. The goal of literal translation is to pursue equivalency with regard to the form, rather than the content, of the text. The underlying assumption is that it is possible to decontextualize certain discourse units, such as words or syntactic units, and find corresponding units in a target language.

The goal of translating with an emphasis on this approach to establishing equivalence to the source text is problematic, however. Nida (1964) describes two distinct types of equivalence: formal and dynamic. *Formal equivalence* refers to equivalence of form and content. *Dynamic equivalence* refers to a target text that yields an effect on a target audience that is similar to the effect of the source text on the original audience. The notion of *formal equivalence* has been debated at every level of linguistic structure.

Perhaps the most basic form in linguistic analysis is the phonological unit. Yet, these are most obviously the units that do not translate from one language to another. The issue of phonological equivalence has often been addressed with regard to translation of poetry, where form and content are inextricably entwined. According to German critic, translator, and historian August Wilhelm Schlegel (1803):

> Since all metrical forms have a definite meaning, and their necessary character in a given language may very well be demonstrated (for unity of form and essence is the goal of all art, and the more they interpenetrate and reflect each other, the higher the perfection achieved), one of the first principles of the art of translation is that a poem should be recreated in the same meter, as far as the nature of the language allows. (from Lefevre 1992, 80)

While a poet might create the sense of a topic through unconscious or intuitive phonological choices, it is critical that translators analyze such forms as a blueprint for the production of the translation (Ray 1976). It is precisely because of the link between form and essence that some question the translatability of poetry (Firth 1951; Jakobson 1959).

In addressing this question, Hatim and Mason cite an example of a Portuguese poem that, in six words, is able to create an image of an evening tryst so embedded in the phonemic form that an attempt to translate it into Spanish was entirely abandoned (1990, 14). Similarly, questions regarding the translatability of poetry between English and American Sign Language (ASL) have been raised by well-known poet and linguist Clayton Valli (personal communication, Jan. 1995). Once again, the question revolves, in part, around the lack of phonological equivalents between languages.

The search for equivalents can also occur at a syntactic level. In a literal translation, the syntactic structure of a sentence would be maintained in the target text. For example, the use of a passive construction in one language might affect the order of the words selected in the target sentence, regardless of whether the target language uses a similar structure to convey passive voice, whether passives are a part of the target language, or whether passives convey different cultural meanings in the target language. In certain East African languages, the use of a passive construction carries a negative meaning with regard to some aspect of what is being said (Filbeck 1972). Clearly, equivalence of form could convey a nonequivalent meaning if the syntactic form of an English passive were translated into such a language.

Perhaps the greatest testament to the problems inherent in the search for formal equivalency is the tendency to view literal translation as a continuum. Rather than discussing literal translation as an issue of right and wrong, the literature is full of references to translations that are more or less literal. For example, Newmark (1981) describes broader categories than does Nida (1964), referring to *semantic* and *communicative* translation, categories less extreme than Nida's notion of *formal* and *dynamic,* in which the former focuses on equivalence of form and content while the latter focuses on equivalence of effect (Hatim and Mason 1990). Similarly, Larson (1984) discusses a continuum of translation ranging from very literal to modified literal, to near idiomatic, to idiomatic, to unduly free (17). The pursuit of equivalence through literal translation seems to represent a goal for translators to establish a neutral position for themselves with regard to their rendered texts. However, Matthew Arnold (1861) aptly expresses the question underlying such attempts: "The translator's 'first duty is to be faithful'; but the question at issue . . . is in what faithfulness consists" (from Lefevre 1992, 68). This is precisely the question underlying the notion of free translation.

Free Translation

Just as the search for neutrality in the translator's influence on the *form* of utterances has been a long-standing issue, so has the question of translation neutrality with regard to the *meaning* of a text.

For example, Cicero described free translation as a translation that is produced in an accessible register of the target language, using as many or as few words as necessary to convey the same sense as the source text (Lefevre 1992, 47). However, focusing on an equivalent meaning is as problematic as the notion of equivalence of form. Nida (1964) has pointed out that the meaning of a text does not only reflect the intent of the originator. Meaning is also influenced by the intent of the recipient of the text, the latter being the focus of dynamic equivalence. Once again, it appears that translators face complex issues in the pursuit of equivalence.

Seleskovitch suggests that word-for-word literal translations are not even possible a majority of the time: "There are words which have direct equivalents in other languages, just as there are words which are 'untranslatable.' This is a cliché which, for once, is true, but with one small correction: untranslatable words are the rule, and words which always have exact translations the exception" (1978, 84). The fact that there simply is not a one-to-one correspondence of words between languages has influenced the search for semantic equivalence. Ray (1976) describes the problem of translating the French pronoun *il* into Bengali, a language with pronouns that do not distinguish gender. She indicates that in order to translate the meaning of the original in an equivalent fashion, one must incorporate the notion of masculine, despite the fact that this might require structural changes. Various approaches to determine the semantic equivalents of words in different languages have been developed to aid the translator in trying to avoid making personal or subjective decisions—to remain neutral and not personally influence the text itself. For instance, Nida (1975) discusses the use of componential analysis in the identification of the contrastive features of certain words for translation purposes.

Another example of the search for equivalent meaning can be seen in the translation of figurative language. Herbert (1968) posits that translators should find equivalent expressions, rather than attempting literal translations of such literary devices as proverbs and metaphors. However, Frishberg (1990) cautions that such choices might be situationally dependent. She describes how the substitution of one literary quote for a quote of similar historical and symbolic meaning in the target language can be appropriate in one circumstance, but not another. She cites an example from Mehta (1971) in which a United Nations interpreter renders a quote from Pushkin within a Russian presentation into an equivalent quote from Shakespeare in the English translation. Frishberg (1990) points out that such a feat would be difficult between English and ASL due to the fact that ASL literature has not traditionally been taught in schools, and thus, ASL literary quotations might not be widely recognized by many audiences (52). Frishberg is not alone in suggesting that situational factors influence such choices in translation (for example, Herbert 1968; Wilss 1982). In fact, the issues that influence translator decisions in the search for equivalence can be described as both numerous and contradictory.

Savory (1968) identifies ten requirements for the production of a good translation. These include the need for a translation to represent both the words and the ideas of the original. As has been discussed here, deferring exclusively to either the words *or* the ideas of a source text can be problematic, while attempting to do both simultaneously exacerbates these problems. What is, perhaps, most interesting about the pursuit of equivalency is that the underlying premise for both literal and free translation appears to be the same: translators should not influence the texts with which they work.

Processes

Much of the research and discussion on interpretation has been influenced by information-processing models that perpetuate the notion of interpreters as machines or conduits (Roy 1989a, 1993). These studies have primarily focused on input (same time + rates), manipulation and segmentation of information (lag + chunking + pauses), and strategies used to cope with information overload.

Examinations of simultaneous interpretation have focused on how interpreters process simultaneous input and output. Welford (1968) described the interpreter's ability to perform these dual tasks by positing that the interpreters actually learn to ignore their own speech in order to focus on the listening task. However, the fact that interpreters initiate repairs, or corrections, within their own utterances indicates that there is attention to their own vocal feedback (Paneth 1957; Gerver 1974a). With regard to the processing of simultaneous input, Pinter (1969) found that subjects with experience interpreting were better able to repeat sentences and answer yes-no questions and Wh-questions that overlapped (or occur simultaneously) with their responses than subjects with no interpreting experience. Wh-questions are those that in English contain interrogative words beginning with "Wh," such as *who, what, when,* and *where.* A study of interpreting students showed that the interpreting students are able to recall and comprehend material that has been interpreted better than material that has been shadowed (repeated in the same language), indicating that it is possible for interpreters to cognitively handle more than one task at a time (Gerver 1974b).

Split attention or split memory is an information-processing approach to understanding interpreters' ability to engage in multiple tasks (Van Hoof 1962). Three-track memory, a notion proposed by Hromosová (1972), is an attempt to account for the interaction between short-term and long-term memory as an interpreter stores the incoming source message, retrieves linguistic knowledge of both languages, and articulates the translation. Numerous models of the interpreting process focus on such issues as input and memory and follow theories of information processing (Richards 1953; Nida 1964; Kade and Cartellieri 1971; Chernov 1973; Gerver 1976; Moser 1978).

Early research regarding simultaneous interpretation (Paneth 1957) addresses the issue of how interpreters manage information. Paneth discusses interpreters' use of lag time, segmentation of the message, and the use of pauses as a time to catch up to the original speaker's point in the presentation. Lag time refers to the time difference between the interpreter hearing the input and producing the translation and, for this reason, has also been referred to as "ear-voice span" (Treisman 1965; Oléron and Nanpon 1965). Treisman examines both shadowing and simultaneous interpreting among noninterpreters, finding that interpreting requires a greater lag time than shadowing. The length of lag time is determined, in part, by the relative difficulty of the input (Oléron and Nanpon 1965). Interestingly, a study of lag time in English–British Sign Language interpretation found that interpreters used a very short lag time (Llewellyn-Jones 1981). In examining ASL-English interpreters, Cokely showed that the length of lag time does influence the quality of the output (Cokely 1992). He indicates that shorter lag times result in a higher number of miscues. Similarly, in a spoken-spoken language interpretation study, Barik (1975) finds that too short a lag yields errors and false starts. Barik also finds that with too long a lag, omissions increase. Because the segmentation of information is critical to accuracy of output, some researchers have focused on how interpreters segment, or organize, information into manageable units.

The manner in which interpreters segment incoming information is inherently linked to the rate at which that information arrives. A study of the effects of input rate on simultaneous interpretation showed that the faster the incoming message, the longer the lag time exhibited by interpreters (Gerver 1969). This study confirmed an earlier estimate of the ideal input rate (Seleskovitch 1965) of approximately 95 to 120 words per minute. The role of lag time in the segmentation of incoming text is addressed by Goldman-Eisler (1972), who finds that frequently lag time consists of syntactic units (such as adverbial expressions). In this study, Goldman-Eisler compares interpreters' segmentations within target output with the original speakers' segmentations in the source message. She finds that very few of the interpreters' chunks match the original segmentation (identity), and that almost half the time interpreters began to translate before a chunk in the source text had been completed (fission). Just over a third of the interpreters' segments involved the linking of two or more chunks from within the source message (fusion). Thus, studies of segmentation and chunking indicate that interpreters influence the structure of the target text.

Research indicates that pauses often serve as unit breaks for interpreters in the attempt to chunk incoming information (Barik 1969; Gerver 1971). Kade and Cartellieri (1971) suggest that interpreters use pauses and redundancies in the original presentation as a time to catch up with the presenter, and Barik (1973) finds that, in practice, interpreters do so. In a study of English-ASL interpretation,

Cokely (1992) finds that 87 percent of pauses are used for this purpose. Pauses have not only been viewed as unit markers, however. Goldman-Eisler (1967, 1968) suggests that within utterances, interpreters use pauses for planning upcoming productions.

Several studies have addressed the ways in which interpreters handle information overload. Interpreters face potential overload problems as a result of the physical and mental demands of interpreting (Brasel 1976). Studies indicate that interpreters do have "adjustment procedures" (Chernov 1969) to assist in such instances of overload. For example, Miller (1964) examines the strategies used by interpreters faced with continuous visual and auditory stimulation. Interpretations include omissions, interruptions of the input, errors, delayings (queueing), systematic omissions (filtering), and reduction in preciseness of output (approximation). Similar categories are identified by Gerver (1969) and Barik (1973). Gerver finds that differences between source and target texts consist of omissions of words, phrases, and longer stretches of text, as well as substitutions of words and phrases. He also finds that target messages include corrections of words and phrases. Barik also identifies specific types of omissions, additions, and substitutions, such as comprehension and delay omissions.

While these studies are experimental in design, Cokely (1982, 1992) has identified similar categories in analyses of interpreters in interaction. In an experimentally designed study of interactive interpreting, Cokely (1982) analyzes the performance of two ASL-English interpreters interpreting medical interviews between a nurse and patient. He identifies four categories of miscues: perception errors, memory errors, semantic errors, and performance errors. In a larger study of ASL-English conference interpreting, Cokely (1992) identifies a taxonomy of interpreter miscues that include not only omissions, additions, and substitutions, but also intrusions and anomalies. Whether experimentally designed or based on natural interaction, studies indicate that information overload influences an interpreter's renditions.

Research regarding the processes involved in interpretation has focused on input, segmentation of texts, and problems associated with information overload. All of these areas relate to the study of information processing. These studies analyze the nature of the process of interpreting as if interpreters are conduits through which linguistic messages are passed. However, the view of interpreters as neutral conduits has, perhaps, inhibited examination of interpreting as it actually occurs: in sociocultural contexts.

The question of equivalence has been at the heart of the field of translation since it was first born. Even before the birth of Christ, the controversy over literal versus free translation existed. While Aristotle encouraged pursuit of "accurate" translations, Cicero attempted to serve the consumers of his text by making dialect and register choices that matched the needs of his audience. Yet, traditionally, much of the research and discussion regarding translation and interpretation has focused on accuracy and equivalence within the product and has addressed the process as if translators are simply human information-processing machines. In recent years, numerous researchers have stressed the need for research regarding the dynamic process of translation as an interactive communication event (Nida 1964; Anderson 1976; Shuy 1987). Perhaps because of its evolution from the disciplines of sociology, anthropology, and linguistics (Shuy 1990), sociolinguistics is a field uniquely designed to meet this need.

Applied Sociolinguistics: Studies of Translation and Interpretation

Concern regarding social and cultural aspects of translation is not a new phenomenon. Many scholars have attempted to incorporate one or another of the many relevant sociocultural aspects of interaction. For example, some earlier studies have considered situational factors (Richards 1953; Catford 1965), style (Wilss 1977), and cultural issues (Vinay and Darbelnet 1958). Some have even prescribed goals for translators and interpreters that incorporate various sociocultural aspects of discourse. For example, Casagrande (1954) indicates the need for translators to balance the pragmatic, semantic, aesthetic, and cultural equivalencies. Similarly, Newmark (1974, 1981) discusses diverse issues with regard to translation, including register, context, jargon, metaphor, and cultural allusions. Nevertheless, in the search for equivalents these various factors, like pragmatic and referential equivalence, often conflict (Hatim and Mason 1990). It is precisely for this reason that the need for a systematic investigation of such factors exists.

With the merging of several relevant disciplines into a new discipline, sociolinguistics, in the early sixties (Shuy 1990), a more cohesive approach to the study of social and cultural issues in translation and interpretation began. Brislin (1976) suggests that sociolinguistic issues are behind what Seleskovitch (1978) describes as the sense that a text conveys beyond the meaning of the words. Moreover, interpretation is not simply the conveyance of meaning between two languages, but rather, between two languages and the communities and cultures of the people who use them (Pergnier 1978). Nida (1964, 1976) suggests that sociolinguistics can contribute to a systematic analysis of the relevant elements in translated texts, including such features as background information about the originator of the message, the text itself, and the recipient of the text (receptor). He posits that "only a sociolinguistic approach to translation is ultimately valid" (1976, 77).

Hatim and Mason have proposed a sociolinguistic model of translation that categorizes issues involved in translation in an effort to impose greater consistency within the discussion of translation (1990). The model is based on three major principles involved in the translation of text: communicative transaction, pragmatic action, and semiotic interaction. *Communicative transaction* encompasses the factors involved in translating the effects of communication. That is, translators must be sensitive to cultural factors and the impact of both the originator and the setting on linguistic output. Cultural differences are also relevant in the notion of *pragmatic action*. Here, the translator must balance the need to incorporate culturally appropriate interactional strategies within both languages. *Semiotic interaction* refers to the need for translators to incorporate equivalent access to ideological aspects of a text. That is, texts often depend on prior textual experiences in order to evoke significant meanings (intertextuality). When recipients of the discourse have not had experience with a particular language and thus, the relevant prior texts, it becomes the responsibility of the translator to provide a translation that allows the recipients to infer the ideological stances intended in the source.

Several early studies in translation attempted to focus on a communication model, which takes into account the perspectives of the original speaker and audience, rather than an information-processing model, which focuses more on the cognitive processes of the interpreter or translator (Nida 1964; Nida and Taber 1969; Kade 1968; Neubert 1968; and Thieberger 1972). Catford (1965) focuses on the impact of situational variables on language use. For Hatim and Mason (1990), communicative transaction specifically refers to language variation. The types of variations addressed include variation with regard to language use (register) and user (dialect). Of particular relevance is research regarding language variation in ASL-English interpretation. Davis (1989, 1990), in an examination of two ASL-English interpreters, found that both interpreters exhibited patterned incorporations of code switching, or switching between two languages; code mixing, or mixing the use of two languages, perhaps within a sentence or combining both codes (such as mouthing English while signing ASL [Lucas and Valli 1992]); and lexical borrowing, or borrowing words from one language while using another. This is attributed, in part, to a unique situational factor often faced by ASL-English interpreters: one of the "monolingual" parties might actually be bilingual. As Davis points out, "In many interpreting situations, the deaf audience has some degree of written or spoken proficiency in the source language (English). In a sense, the interpretation is needed not because the deaf audience members don't understand English, but because they cannot hear it" (1990, 319).

Because some deaf participants might be fluent in English, a unique form of interpreting has evolved for use by interpreters working with such a population: transliteration. Transliteration has traditionally referred to the translation between English and a signed code for English.[1] In an analysis of a transliterator providing access between a hearing teacher and class and a deaf student in a university course, Winston (1989) and Siple (1995) found that the transliteration actually consists of not only "English-like signing," but has some of both English-like and ASL-like linguistic features. The findings from these studies indicate the importance of sociolinguistic research regarding aspects of the *communicative transaction* in translation.

In a discussion of pragmatic issues to be considered by translators, Hatim and Mason (1990) address such issues as illocutionary force of source and target texts—for example, the function of the text (to request, to demand, etc.) perhaps directly or indirectly—as well as structural features such as the regulation of turn-taking, or the use of pauses and intonation to hold or yield one's turn in a spoken conversation (Sacks, Schegloff, and Jefferson 1974), and the occurrence of adjacency pairs, which are two-part sequences that occur in conversations, as in greetings (e.g., "Hello" is followed by the response, "Hello"; or "How are you?" by "Fine" in English) (Schegloff and Sacks 1973). In a study of interpreters in legal settings, Berk-Seligson (1990) found that interpreters would sometimes change the pragmatic meaning of source utterances, for example, by using a different grammatical case in the interpretation from that used in the original. In some cases, this left interlocutors with two different perceptions of the interaction.

The presence of interpreters does more than influence interlocutors' perceptions of an interaction, however. Zimmer (1989) examined the pragmatic influence of an ASL-English interpreter by analyzing the audiotaped English portion of an interpreted interview. She found that the English portion of the discourse included longer pauses, limited back-channeling, and an unusually high frequency of fillers (apparently the result of participant discomfort with the long pauses). While these findings indicate that the presence of the interpreter influenced the structure of the interpreted interaction, Zimmer points out that the interlocutors' perceptions of one another might also be influenced by the unique features of the interpreted discourse. Thus, a sociolinguistic examination of the pragmatic features of interpreted encounters indicates that interpreters are not entirely neutral with regard to their influence on the perceptions of the interlocutors. In a study of turn-taking in an interpreted interaction, Roy finds that interpreters clearly influence the flow of the interaction itself.

Roy (1989a, 1993) examined the role of an ASL-English interpreter in the turn exchanges of an interpreted interaction between a university student and his professor. She found that during the overlapping dialogue the interpreter employed several strategies, including controlling the floor, retaining part of a message for later, and ignoring the overlap and interpreting neither of the utterances. She concluded that the interpreter is clearly an active participant in the interaction. Sociolinguistic analyses regarding pragmatic actions also reveal important empirically based information about interpreted interactions.

The factors considered by Hatim and Mason (1990) to be semiotic in nature include such issues as discourse genre, the texture of the discourse, and the relationship of a current text to prior texts. These features, as relatively intentional strategies (as opposed to dialect, for instance), are considered to be stylistic issues in translation. Winston (1993) provides an example of the importance of discourse texture in interpretation between ASL and English. In her study of the use of space in an ASL lecture, Winston identifies spatial strategies within the lecture that create cohesion within the text. For example, Winston describes how the lecturer creates maps in the space surrounding him and later refers to those spaces (for example, by pointing to them) without explicit reference. She indicates that interpreters must understand the cohesive devices of both languages in order to appropriately translate the meaning of a text. Clearly, sociolinguistic analyses of both interpretation and the discourse of the languages being interpreted are critical contributions to the understanding and evaluation of translated and interpreted texts.

In an examination of the impact of stylistic strategies selected by interpreters, Berk-Seligson (1990) found that court interpreters often translate fragmented source utterances into narrative renditions. In addition, she examined the impact of the inclusion or exclusion of politeness markers in interpretations presented to "mock" jurors and found that even among different groupings of jurors (based on mono- versus bilingual status), the perceptions of witnesses and attorneys were clearly influenced by the interpretations. In an earlier study of ASL-English interpretation, Cokely (1982) reported similar findings. He analyzed the perceptions of the target recipients of interpretations of a single lecturer, and found both distinctions and limitations in how ASL-English interpreters convey speaker affect. In an interactive analysis of spoken-spoken language interpreted interviews, Wadensjö (1992) examined the function of interpreters' choices. She found that when interpreters produced renditions (interpretations of others' utterances), they often altered the renditions for specific purposes. For example, one interpreter provided a rendition of an interviewee response regarding why he had moved from his home country, but omitted specific information about the dates. This information was not apparently relevant to the interviewer, who was interested only in the reasons for the move. Thus, situated analysis of omissions (what Wadensjö calls *reduced renditions*) is in keeping with interactive goals.

While sociolinguistic issues have been recognized as pertinent to the field of translation since long before the term *sociolinguistics* existed, the emergence of sociolinguistics as a field with its own theoretical frameworks and methodological practices has provided a means for the systematic investigation of sociocultural issues impacting translation and interpretation. Although much work remains to be done, one interesting phenomenon that is apparent from the sociolinguistic studies discussed here is that the interpreters under investigation have clearly influenced the interpreted encounters in which they work in all three areas identified by Hatim and Mason (1990): communicative, pragmatic, and semiotic. Yet, as Hatim and Mason point out, while some of these influences are inherent to the process of translation, others appear to be particularly significant to interpretation. Thus, while the processes of translation and interpreting have much in common, it is worth noting some of the differences that result from the different modes that translators and interpreters face in their work.

The Relevance of Mode

In discussion of the impact of working within different modes, Nida (1976) considers the written and oral mediums to have a significant impact on the form of the source and target messages. In addition to the written and spoken modes, there is yet a third medium to be addressed: signing. Not only can a distinction be made between translation and interpretation, but also between interpreting with spoken languages and signed languages.

It has been said that the prerequisites to good translation and interpretation are the same. Both require the understanding of the sense of an original utterance and its function within the context in which it occurs (Seleskovitch 1978). However, the amount of time allowed for the production of a rendition has a tremendous impact on the nature of these two distinct processes. For example, because translation conveys messages from and to the written medium, the translator can refer to the original at any time (Wilss 1982). Cokely has outlined the implications of this time factor as follows:

1. The text is permanently at the translator's disposal; thus, the translator is able to review the text in its entirety before beginning to translate;

2. The text and its translation are written; the translator can refer back to previously translated sections and passages;

3. The translation can be reviewed; the translator has the option of seeking feedback from both bilingual and monolingual reviewers;

4. The translated text can be reviewed; the translator can make corrections. (1992, 16)

As Cokely indicates, translators can check their work (themselves or with assistance) and can see the whole source prior to translation with the option to refer back to past portions at any time. On the other hand, an interpreter must make fast decisions regarding the meaning of a text, without necessarily knowing the author's intent or meaning in advance. In translating into a language that denotes gender in pronouns from one that does not, a translator can read ahead to determine the gender of the pronoun's antecedent. However, an interpreter is left with the option of asking the speaker, guessing (risking error), or waiting for the information to be made clear (risking falling behind). An interpreter cannot refer back to prior portions of the discourse and rarely has the opportunity to incorporate feedback from others or to review his or her work before it is made public. Moreover, an interpreter cannot make use of reference materials (such as dictionaries), as translators do (Van Dam 1989). As a result of the time factor, Seleskovitch (1977) suggests that a fundamental distinction between translation and interpretation is that while both aim to convey an equivalent sense of the source message, translators have the time to address linguistic meaning whereas interpreters do not.

A benefit that interpreters receive from the time factor is that they generally have the opportunity to meet the source and recipients of their work. Translators often do not have this opportunity (Landsberg 1976; Wilss 1982). Furthermore, Seleskovitch (1977) suggests that the time limitation faced by simultaneous interpreters can actually be beneficial in the sense that the interaction of time pressures and short-term memory constraints require the interpreter to let go of linguistic forms while retaining the sense that is left behind.

While translation and interpretation can be seen to differ as a result of time constraints, the time factor can also differ with regard to the nature of interpretation. Interpreters can work either consecutively or simultaneously. In consecutive interpretation, the interpreter receives the source message first, and then renders an interpretation of it. The source message can be presented in parts or as a whole. Consecutive interpretation allows the interpreter a certain amount of input (and thus, an opportunity to make closure) as well as the opportunity to take notes. With simultaneous interpretation the interpreter must render a source message, producing a rendition even while listening to the ongoing message, and continue to interpret until the source message stops. Although consecutive interpreting is often considered to be the more accurate of the two, simultaneous interpreting is much more time efficient. It is for this reason that simultaneous interpreting first came into wider use at the Nuremberg Trials in the late forties (Ramler 1988).

While simultaneous interpreting is relatively new with regard to spoken language interpretation, it is more or less traditional in signed language interpretation. Although some of the historical developments within the sibling fields of spoken and signed language interpretation are distinct, many aspects of the tasks are quite similar. Because this study will address ASL-English interpretation, it is worth noting the similarities and differences between signed and spoken language interpretation.

In large part, the similarities relate to the issue that is common to interpreting and translation; that is, both require an understanding of the sense of the source text. In addition, both signed language and spoken language interpreters must deal with time factors not faced by translators in the written mode. The simultaneous and consecutive approaches to interpretation are used in both spoken and signed language interpretation. Moreover, concerns regarding the rendering of equivalent messages without intervening in the interaction are common to both forms of interpreting (Roberts 1987). Because of the fact that these issues are similar, many of them have already been addressed.

Several differences exist between the two modes of interpreting as well. One difference is the result of the fact that some of the consumers of signed language interpretation might actually be bilingual individuals who simply do not have access to both languages in face-to-face interaction. In spoken language interpretation, if one or more interlocutors are bilingual (in the languages of the encounter) they are able to access both the original utterance and the interpreted rendition. For Deaf interlocutors who are bilingual in ASL and English, this type of access is not necessarily possible. This difference between signed language and spoken language interpreting underscores the fact that signed language interpreters often work between different modes. That is, where most spoken language interpreting involves the rendering of messages between two spoken languages, most signed language interpreting actually involves one signed and one spoken language. Thus, the circumstances faced by signed language interpreters are not only interlingual, but intermodal as well (Wilss 1982). This modality difference has potentially influenced expectations of signed language interpreters. Since one mode is visual and the other auditory, it can appear as if there is no interference between the two. However, both the source and the target are distinct languages that require the interpreter's attention. Nevertheless, since one of the languages requires that the interpreter watch the incoming message, signed language interpreters are not in a position to take notes when following the consecutive method.

Aside from issues of modality, there are two additional areas in which signed and spoken language interpretation differ. According to Roberts (1987), spoken language interpreters have historically been treated with some prestige. Conversely, signed language interpreters have had to deal with outdated assumptions that signed languages are primitive nonlinguistic systems. Further, according to Roberts, spoken language interpreters have often worked in conferences and other high-profile settings, while signed language interpreters worked for many years in small group settings.

It has become clear that while both translation and interpretation share many features, the differences between the two are significant with regard to the actual tasks. Similarly, while spoken and signed language interpretation share many features, significant differences between them exist as well. These differences will be relevant throughout the analysis of ASL-English interpreters. Nevertheless, one similarity, the issue of neutrality, is particularly relevant to the task of interpretation. In light of this, it is important to elaborate on a condition that all interpreters inherently confront and that invariably affects the progression of the intended dyadic structure of interpreted encounters: interpreter neutrality is a paradox.

The Interpreter's Paradox

The goal of neutrality is a topic that has pervaded much of the research and discussion of translation and interpreting. In part, this is the result of professionalization. It is also partly due to the "third

party" status of interpreters and the resulting perception of interpreters as mediators. The desire for neutrality (i.e., equivalence) in
translation has been shown to be an underlying factor for both sides
of the traditional "literal versus free" translation controversy. Furthermore, notions of neutrality seem to be linked to assumptions
implicit in early research on interpreting that followed information-
processing paradigms. However, the advent of sociolinguistics has
provided tools that allow for more systematic investigation of interpreting within the social and cultural contexts in which it occurs.
Sociolinguistic investigations of interpreted encounters have raised
serious questions regarding the notion of interpreters as neutral conduits. If interpreters have the goal of remaining neutral, this research
suggests a contradiction between the goal and the reality of interpreted encounters.

Over time, ASL-English interpreters have attempted to cope
with this issue in different ways. Witter-Merithew (1986) describes
four models of the interpreters' role that seem to have emerged as a
result of the contradiction between interpreters' goals and reality:
helper, conduit, communication facilitator, and bilingual, bicultural
specialist. The helper model refers to a time when there was no professional organization for interpreters, and most people doing the interpreting were hearing friends and relatives of Deaf people who had
some fluency in both languages. The conduit model projects the interpreter as machinelike and came about during early stages of professionalization. As interpreters attempted to fulfill this machine
model, problems arose with regard to responsibility for the quality
of interpretations and negative consumer perceptions of interpreters. These problems led to the emergence of the communication
facilitator model. According to Roy (1989a, 1993), despite minor
changes in terms of language attitudes (for example, increasing respect for ASL) and expectations of interpreters' linguistic expertise,
the communication facilitator model is very similar to the conduit
model. In keeping with the historical progression discussed earlier,
the most recent model, the interpreter as bilingual, bicultural specialist, considers situational and cultural factors as relevant to the
interpreting task.

Despite the progression of these models historically, ASL-English interpreters do not always function consistently within one model. Roy (1993) suggests that many interpreters still follow the conduit model. McIntire and Sanderson (1995) suggest that situational factors can influence which model an interpreter follows, pointing out that the models are descriptions of practice rather than proactive prescriptions. They argue that for twenty years consumers have not received consistency in the approach interpreters follow.

Interpreters are not the only professionals who face what appear to be contradictions within their work. Researchers interested in studying human behavior have always faced the difficulty of trying to examine the natural, everyday behavior of people when the presence of a researcher is not a part of everyday life. Labov (1972) describes this dilemma within sociolinguistic fieldwork, calling it the Observer's Paradox. Sociolinguistic field-workers might aim to collect discourse as it occurs in daily interaction. However, daily interaction does not include the presence of a researcher. Thus, reality is at odds with the professional's goal. This is similar to the situation faced by interpreters. Interpreters have expressed the goal of not influencing the form, content, structure, and outcomes of interactive discourse, but the reality is that interpreters, by their very presence, influence the interaction.

Interpreters are not merely impartial intermediaries facilitating dyadic interaction. Instead, interpreters function as participants within the discourse, regulating turns (Roy 1989, 1993) and altering contributions in ways that are designed to meet interactional goals established by the participants (Wadensjö 1992). An updated view of interpreters in communication events is proposed in figure 1.1 (p. 24). The three solid lines in figure 1.1 indicate that there is a primary connection among all the participants. The interpreter *and* the participants are all actively engaged in the communicative event. Nevertheless, if interpreters are active participants while rendering the words of others, their participation still seems to be different from that of other participants. Wadensjö describes this seeming contradiction in her description of interpreted encounters: "The whole interaction is a peculiar type of three-party talk with the [interpreter]

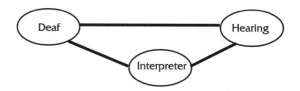

Figure 1.1. Triadic view of interpreting.

as one interactant" (1992, 273). Further investigation regarding the interpreter's contributions to interactive discourse can assist in clarifying this peculiarity.

The fact that interpreters are supposed to provide access to an interaction of which they are, in reality, a part (the Interpreter's Paradox) raises serious questions regarding interpreting practice. If interpreters are participants in an interaction, should they be as free as other participants to influence the structure and outcomes of the encounter? Or, should interpreters begin to recognize the ways in which they can minimize their influence, just as many researchers attempt to cope with the Observer's Paradox. Baker-Shenk (1991) addresses this issue with clear conviction, indicating that there is no such thing as "neutrality" for interpreters. She concludes that it is imperative for interpreters to learn the impact of their choices and to make responsible decisions.

Sociolinguistics provides the theoretical and methodological tools with which to examine the ways in which interpreters influence interactive discourse. This study consists of an examination of the ways in which participants frame interpreted encounters and the function of interpreters' contributions to interpreted medical interviews. To begin the investigation of the influences ASL-English interpreters have on interactive medical discourse, it is first necessary to understand what makes this genre of discourse unique.

2

Analyzing Interpreted Medical Interviews

IN ORDER to examine ways in which ASL-English interpreters influence interactive discourse, it is important to recognize that not all interactive discourse is identical. Interactive discourse, as it is used here, refers to dialogic or multiparty interactions. Certain aspects of interaction are applicable to most encounters, while others are situationally determined and as varied as the background and goals of the participants. For instance, conversation analysts, in the ethnomethodological tradition of Garfinkel (1967, 1974), have identified stable, structural features of interactive discourse, such as adjacency pairs (Schegloff and Sacks 1973) and the organization of turn-taking (Sacks, Schegloff, and Jefferson 1974). An adjacency pair is a feature of conversation that has two parts, such as a greeting followed by a greeting or a question followed by an answer. These stable, structural features can be found in one form or another in almost all interactional discourse.

Hymes (1972) has identified consistent features of communicative events, indicating that setting, participants, goals, and discourse genre are some of the important components of interactive discourse. Taking an anthropological perspective, Hymes's work addresses the need to understand the larger context in which interaction occurs, as well as features that vary from one interaction to another. For example, Hymes identifies a taxonomy regarding interactive discourse, including the *speech situation*, the *speech event*, and the *speech act*. Speech act refers to the function of a particular utterance, such as a joke. The speech act takes place within a particular speech event, such as a conversation. This event takes place within a larger speech situation, such as a party (Hymes 1972, 56). This is one way in which Hymes is able to examine both the larger context and the local context within an interaction.

Interactional sociolinguists have studied how people understand (or misunderstand) one another in specific interactions. Evidence regarding the situated nature of interactions and the potentially significant influence of such contextual clues as code choice (e.g., choice of language or dialect) can be found in Gumperz (1982). In one example, Gumperz demonstrates that when a speaker chooses to switch from one dialect to another, that code switch can be interpreted by different people to mean different things:

> Following an informal graduate seminar at a major university, a black student approached the instructor, who was about to leave the room accompanied by several other black and white students, and said:
>   a. Could I talk to you for a minute? I'm gonna apply for a fellowship and I was wondering if I could get a recommendation?
>   The instructor replied:
>   b. O.K. Come along to the office and tell me what you want to do. As the instructor and the rest of the group left the room, the black student said, turning his head ever so slightly to the other students:
>   c. Ahma git me a gig!
>   (Rough gloss: "I'm going to get myself some support.")
>   (Gumperz 1982, 30)

Gumperz indicates that the code switch from Standard English to Black dialect was interpreted by some to indicate a rejection of both the white instructor and the institution. Others, however, interpreted the change in code choice to suggest that the student was addressing other students in the group, demonstrating that he was merely going along with the system, as many do in a white-dominated environment. A variety of social factors influence the interpretation of this interaction, including the time, people, and location in which it occurred.

Given that interactive discourse is highly influenced by the situation in which it occurs, it is important to narrow studies of interpretation to specific genres of discourse. This allows specific encounters to be analyzed with regard to the same macro- and micro-analytical issues that have been applied to analyses of noninterpreted discourse. As a result of the serious nature of the outcomes associated with the genre, and despite methodological challenges in collecting the necessary data, the focus here will be on interpreted medical interviews.

Interviews As a Discourse Genre

Among the various types of interactive discourse, interviews constitute a particular genre of discourse. Interviews serve a variety of functions, including elicitation of information for research purposes or for news reports. In general, interviews involve two or more people. The interviewer generally has more control over the structure of the interaction than the interviewee (for example, control over turn-taking). On the other hand, the interviewee has knowledge or information that is sought by the interviewer.

With regard to institutional interviews, Labov (1984) discusses the existence of asymmetry between interviewer and interviewee. Moreover, he indicates that the structure of such interviews is relatively fixed, as compared with other types of interaction, both in terms of topic selection and question-response format. Hohenberg (1983), McDowell (1986), and Mischler (1986) discuss media interviews, information interviews, and research interviews, respectively, indicating that in all three cases the interviewer maintains some measure of control over the structure of the interaction. Nevertheless, it is worth noting that the ways in which interviewers manifest their control might vary. While media interviewers are generally encouraged to thoroughly research their topic in advance and prepare a well-organized sequence of questions, a technical writer interviewing for information is likely to follow a more spontaneous question format based on interviewee responses rather than adhering to a preset sequence of inquiry. Despite differences in approach, the relatively fixed and formal structure of interviews as described by Labov (1984) remains consistent.

The formal nature of interviews, and their effectiveness as a means of eliciting information, has been of interest to sociolinguists since the first sociolinguistic interviews were conducted almost thirty years ago. Shuy, Wolfram, and Riley (1968), Labov (1972), Kibrik (1977), and Briggs (1986) were among the first to address such issues. In a more recent discussion of the sociolinguistic interview, Schiffrin (1993) applies discourse analysis techniques in her analysis of a sociolinguistic interview. She concludes that just as sociolinguists recognize variations in speaker style, sociolinguistic studies can "incorporate the idea that identity is dynamic and is mutually constitutive with the organization of talk" (259). Schiffrin points out that people quite possibly demonstrate a similar dynamism with regard to their identity and participant structures within other types of interviews, not just in sociolinguistic interviews. The issue of how participants respond to interview discourse has been critical in analyses of medical interviews.

Analyses of Medical Interview Discourse

In general, a medical interview can be described as a professional interview, similar to those conducted by attorneys and accountants. Donaghy describes medical interviews as a type of diagnostic interview, "an interview between an interviewer who possesses special knowledge and skills and a respondent who provides information so that the interviewer can analyze a specific situation or problem" (1984, 301). The purpose of most medical interviews is for the interviewee, or patient, to consult an expert in order to relieve some physical ailment. As a result, the focus of such interviews is on eliciting a medical history by collecting information about the current illness and symptoms as well as the past medical history (MacKinnon and Michels 1971). The elicitation of this information is critical to the effective diagnosis of a patient's condition. However, as Shuy (1972, 1976, 1983) and others since have discovered through applied sociolinguistic analyses, the elicitation of such information in medical interviews is often problematic.

Problems associated with doctor-patient communication have been attributed to many factors, including differences in language, culture, background knowledge, and goals. These differences have led to further problems, including ineffective medical policies and unnecessary operations. Perhaps because of the serious implications resulting from problems in doctor-patient communication, research has focused on identifying the causes for the problems in this particular setting.

Many researchers have studied the effects of doctors' use of medical jargon on a patient's ability to comprehend medical discourse. For example, Shuy (1972, 1976, 1979, and 1983), Ford (1976), and Fisher (1983) address problems found in the use of specialized vocabulary. Words relating to anatomy and illness are not the only kind of terminology that creates problems in understanding, however. The application of everyday terms to specialized purposes is also cited as causing confusion for some patients. For example, the term "infection" has a meaning in everyday language that might not extend to the description of such ailments as pneumonia or blood poisoning. Yet, according to Shuy (1972), medical specialists use this everyday term in reference to these ailments.

Research also indicates that problems in communication are not limited to patient confusion. A doctor's inability to understand patients' ways of speaking can cause communication problems in the medical interview as well. In recent work, Bonanno (1995) analyzes the unbalanced use of approximators by doctors and patients. Bonanno's study of approximators is based on a study of the typology of hedges, which are words or phrases that tend to weaken or qualify a statement ("It was *sort of* ugly") or a speaker's relationship to it (*"I think* she is coming") (Prince et al. 1982). Approximators are a subcategory of hedges that "create fuzziness within the propositional content" (Bonanno 1995, 46), for example, describing a symptom as "sort of a spinning sensation" (132). Bonanno finds that patients use approximators more than twice as often as doctors. Bonanno suggests that since patients' use of approximators can leave the doctor confused, patients who answer questions more directly, even by indicating when solicited information is unknown, will likely experience more successful medical interviews and diagnoses.

Communication breakdowns are not limited to vocabulary choices. Shuy (1972, 1976, 1983) discusses ways in which cultural differences create barriers in doctor-patient understanding. For example, Shuy (1972) discusses the use of questions that reflect the doctors' middle-class lifestyles, rather than the reality of most patients' lives. A question about exercise specifically asked patients about how much time they spend exercising (i.e., jogging or playing tennis), when most of these patients spent over twenty minutes a day walking and were not concerned about such issues. Similarly, Mishler (1984) discusses how the distinct voices of the medical world and the "lifeworld" interact within doctor-patient communication. His analysis, like those of Tannen and Wallat and Cicourel, indicates that the patient and the doctor bring different experiences and backgrounds to the medical interview.

Cicourel and Tannen and Wallat discuss differences in register use between doctors and patients. For example, the presence of the mother in a pediatric interview causes the doctor to shift between registers and interrupts the flow of the medical examination (Tannen and Wallat 1982, 1983, 1987, 1993). Cicourel compares a doctor's factual notes from a medical interview with the imprecise and emotional language actually provided by the patient. In this study the shift in registers was shown to result in factual errors in documentation (1983).

Bonanno (1995) and Fisher (1983) both discuss the fact that doctors and patients are attending to different tasks. For example, while doctors conduct interviews in a familiar environment, using familiar language, and following their own busy schedules, patients must face unfamiliar surroundings and unknown jargon, and are generally in the weakened position of being ill at the time of the interview. Moreover, while a doctor is seeing one of many people with a given condition, patients might be facing a decision that could impact their daily routine or even their lives (Fisher 1983, 153). The different tasks faced by doctors and patients can influence who controls the interview (Bonanno 1995).

Asymmetry within the Medical Interview

The medical interview is often an asymmetrical interchange. Most research indicates that doctors control the interaction, as evidenced

by a variety of linguistic features, including topic initiation and regulation of turn-taking.

Shuy (1979) suggests that the situation of doctors' controlling
medical interviews is analogous to teachers' managing classroom
discourse or police investigators' running interrogations. Shuy and
others have found that professionals' control of an interaction can
negatively impact the effectiveness of communication. Skopek
(1975) found that the structural features controlled by doctors include openings, closings, turn-taking, and topic initiation. In an examination of topic initiation by doctors, Shuy (1983) indicates that
of three physicians who control the selection of topic, the one who
uses a more casual conversational style elicits information from his
patient more successfully. Cicourel (1983) supports the contention
that misunderstandings between doctors and patients can result
from a patient's weakened ability to communicate.

Despite the fact that doctors have been found to have the more
powerful role in medical interviews, patients influence medical discourse as well. For instance, work described earlier by Tannen and
Wallat (1982, 1983, 1987, 1993) indicates that the presence of the
parent in a pediatric examination has an impact on the doctor's discourse. Aronsson (1991) reports similar findings, indicating that a
mother's use of pronouns to refer to her child affects the involvement of the child, casting the patient as a side-participant or a non-
participant in the interaction (Aronsson 1991, 71).

West (1983) and Frankel (1984) examine the question-answer
format within medical interviews and suggest that the asymmetrical role is not simply assumed by the doctor. West suggests that patients who stammer while asking questions demonstrate that both
patients and doctors contribute to the asymmetry of medical interview discourse, since stammering might represent a less confident
or powerful way of speaking. Still, Shuy (1983) finds that while some
patients attempt to interrupt doctors, more often than not the attempts fail to elicit a turn. As Shuy points out, since patients are the
ones with the information critical to the diagnosis and treatment of
medical problems, doctors would better elicit such information by

not following the traditional structure of medical interviews. Instead, Shuy suggests that doctors use a more conversational type of discourse, encouraging patients to share the information so critical to the doctors' task.

Interpreters in Medical Settings

A special package designed for medical practitioners who might be working with Deaf patients was developed in the late seventies. In this package, DiPietro (1979) offers suggestions for working with sign language interpreters. Medical practitioners are encouraged to communicate directly with deaf patients, in terms of both eye gaze and pronominal reference. Interestingly, only two of thirty-three pages are devoted to working with interpreters. The majority of the information presented by DiPietro assumes that no interpreter will be present and that medical practitioners are primarily hearing and have little experience with either the American Deaf community or ASL. Perhaps researchers share this assumption, for very little research has been conducted in the area of interpreting in medical settings.

Cicourel (1981) and Cokely (1982) address the issue of problematic doctor-patient communication as it extends to interpreted medical interviews. For example, Cicourel examines a doctor-patient interview in which a third person is acting as interpreter. As in his work on uninterpreted medical interviews, Cicourel finds that as a result of control over the interactive exchange, the doctor might not be effective in eliciting patient information.

Cokely (1982) conducted an experimental study in which a hearing nurse interviewed a Deaf patient on two separate occasions. In each case the interview was interpreted by certified, professional ASL-English interpreters. Cokely found that four factors interfered with communication, beyond the normal communication problems addressed in literature on doctor-patient communication: perception errors, memory errors, semantic errors, and performance errors. Perception errors occur when the interpreter believes he/she understood an original utterance (such as a proper name), but, in fact, did not understand it correctly. Memory errors are identifiable when small portions of the original utterance unintentionally fail to appear in the interpreter's rendition. When an interpreter incorrectly uses certain lexical items or syntactic structures within a target language rendition, Cokely terms this a semantic error. Finally, performance errors include extraneous behaviors or errors in the production of the utterance. For example, a false start with no repair can appear to the receiver as if it were a word different from the one intended. In Cokely's example, the interpreter fingerspells the name of a medication, interrupts that to spell the abbreviation of the term, then attempts to spell the name of the medication a second time: "E-D-E-T-H-O-S-D-E-S-D-E-T-H-O-S-T-A-B-E-T-H-A-L." Cokely points out that without any pauses or repairs, it looks as though the name of the medication is "edethosdesdethostabethal," when in fact the medication being referred to is "diethylstilbestrol" (9). Cokely concludes that potential communication problems specific to interpreting increase the likelihood of miscommunication in medical interviews.

In a study of spoken language interpreted medical interviews, Wadensjö (1992) examined twenty Swedish-Russian interpreted encounters, thirteen of which occurred in medical settings. Wadensjö refers to Swedish studies of interpreted medical interviews that indicate that interpreted conversations are unnatural dyadic communication (Kulick 1982), based, in part, on findings of unusual backchanneling in the interpreted interviews (Englund Dimitrova 1991). Wadensjö herself finds that interpreters function not only as translators, but as negotiators or coordinators of the interactive discourse.

Interpreted medical settings are influenced not only by linguistic issues. Prince (1986) analyzed medical interviews between English-speaking doctors and Spanish-speaking patients. In addition to those interviews that were conducted in Spanish, Prince discusses the interviews for which a clinic employee or patient's friend or relative served as an interpreter. She concludes that the doctors lacked both linguistic and cultural awareness of these patients and that this negatively influenced their ability to provide effective medical care.

Interactive ASL-English Interpreting in Medical Interviews
Collecting linguistic data from medical interviews is never a simple matter, and the need for the presence of video cameras to capture the signed portion of the interpreted encounter makes data collection even more challenging. These challenges range from human issues, such as informant privacy, to technological constraints such as how many cameras are needed to capture the signed utterances of both the Deaf participant and the interpreter. These issues influence the choice of data to be analyzed, as outlined below.

The Data
In initial data gathering, more than eight hours of interpreted interactions were collected. This data consists of two types. One type of data was collected through live videotaping of the interactive encounters, with the researcher present as a technician to run the camera, check the lighting and sound, and so forth. The second type of data was elicited by contacting interpreter education programs. These programs were asked to suggest or submit videotapes of interpreted encounters. Both types of data have advantages and disadvantages.

Videotaped Data
Videotaping interpreted encounters involves problems of both a human and a technological nature. These issues include the intrusiveness of the recording equipment, the limitations of the recording equipment, and the added risk to informants' confidentiality as a result of the type of recording being made.

Technologically, it is necessary to set up video equipment that will record both the visual and acoustic linguistic information. Thus, lighting, sound, and physical space might need to be manipulated in an effort to record "naturally occurring" data. Clearly, the presence of a researcher is enough to alter the natural flow of an interaction, what Labov (1972) terms the Observer's Paradox. Add to that the presence of, and space occupied by, the video equipment and the logistical manipulations of participants and equipment, and the result is somewhat less than ideal. Wadensjö, in her study of spoken language interpreted encounters, describes this as problematic and avoids using video recorders for this very reason (1992, 58).

Aside from the intrusive nature of video technology, the problem of recording the necessary data also exists. While an audio recorder is capable of capturing all of the sounds in a given environment, albeit in an overlapping way, a video camera is necessarily limited to a restricted scope of "vision." That is, the only way to record all interactants is to be far from the center of events, and to risk capturing some participants from behind. Neither of these conditions is conducive to the work of the signed language linguist, who requires access to detailed manual, body, and facial articulations in order to accurately transcribe the linguistic data. One solution to this problem is to use additional video cameras. However, this adds to the level of intrusiveness, and is difficult to coordinate for later viewing and transcription. A more realistic solution is to adapt the single camera to the extent possible, sometimes risking the loss of valuable pieces of information as participants move away from one another and force the technician to select which parts of the interaction to record.

An additional problem inherent in the collection of visual data is the issue of informant confidentiality. Although voice recognition is always a possibility with audio recorded data, video recordings leave no question as to the identity of participants involved in such research (Winston and Ball 1994). When collecting data in confidential settings, such as medical interviews, many potential informants are uncomfortable with the prospect of videotaping these encounters. Especially problematic is the need to maintain privacy while attempting to publish transcriptions of the ASL data. Although conventions have been established for transcribing ASL through the use of English glosses and other mechanisms, often still photographs are used to most accurately represent the linguistic forms under discussion (for examples, see Locker McKee 1992; Winston 1993).

Finally, an unavoidable issue with regard to the collection of live videotaped ASL data is the influence of the technician and setting on the participants' language choice. Lucas (1994) and Lucas and Valli (1989, 1991, 1992) discuss sociolinguistic factors that influence language use among native ASL signers. They argue that certain situational factors, such as formality of the situation or the linguistic background of interlocutors, can influence whether or not Deaf native ASL signers actually produce ASL or a type of contact signing.

In their examination of language contact situations, Lucas and Valli found that what had previously been labeled Pidgin Sign English was not, in fact, a pidgin, but rather, a form of contact signing. Moreover, they found that hearing or deaf status is not the influencing factor regarding the output of contact signing. Rather, sociolinguistic factors, such as language background, had a greater influence on language choice. For example, Deaf informants signed ASL with hearing native ASL users in some settings and used contact signing with other native Deaf signers in other situations.

The contact variety of signing described in Lucas and Valli (1992) includes unique lexical forms as well as morphological and syntactic structures. Lexical signs are used in contact signing to represent English prepositions, conjunctions, and so forth. In addition, mouthing, whispering, or even audible voicing of English words occurs sometimes with and sometimes without accompanying signs. Fingerspelled signs used to represent English inflectional and derivational morphemes such as #ING and #MENT are one type of morphological structure found in contact signing (84). Other morphological structures include the use of some ASL verb inflections and classifier predicates. Interestingly, Lucas and Valli also found some ASL indicating verbs are produced without subject and/or object marking in the contact variety. Lucas and Valli also discuss a variety of syntactic structures found within the contact variety of signing in their data. Some of these structures include the use of prepositions, "that" constructions, and sentence constructions that follow English word order. Some of the syntactic structures found in the contact signing followed neither English nor ASL word order. Clearly, contact signing differs linguistically from standard ASL.

Lucas and Valli's findings have implications regarding the collection of data in medical settings. Whatever influences the medical settings and interpreter's background might have on the Deaf participant's language choice (as well as the influence that the setting and participants all have on each other's language choices), the presence of the researcher and video camera clearly lessen the likelihood of collecting ASL, rather than contact signing, data from the Deaf participants. The extent to which code switching within the ASL discourse might differ without the presence of researcher and camera cannot be determined. Nevertheless, this is an especially relevant issue since ASL-English interpreters are expected to use language "most readily understood by the person(s) whom they serve" (RID Code of Ethics). Thus, it would be useful to have the opportunity to analyze data that was clearly not influenced by a researcher and the presence of the intrusive video camera.

Prerecorded Data

The second type of data collected for this study came from interpreter education programs. The data consist primarily of interpreting students engaged in interpreting role plays simulating a variety of real-life encounters. Most of the participants are Deaf and hearing interlocutors who have been invited to the interpreting program to interact in a real or imagined area of expertise. Because the resulting scenarios are mock interviews, the interpreting students have the opportunity to interpret these interactions with less concern about questions and errors that arise as part of the learning process.

The benefits regarding this prerecorded data are twofold. First, the student interpreters and the deaf and hearing participants have all given permission after the fact for the videotapes to be used for research purposes. That is, during the encounters, no researcher was present and participants had no knowledge or expectation that the videotape would be used for the purpose of research. Second, since videotaping these interactions was a part of the classroom routine, the video camera was not perceived as an outside intrusion. Moreover, because the original purpose of videotaping was for students to have the opportunity to observe and critique their interpreting performance, the videotapes were designed to include all of the participants in the recording for its duration. In some cases, this was accomplished through careful arrangement of participant seating. In other cases, a two-camera simultaneous recording was made using a device that allows participants to face one another while appearing on the recording via a split screen. Because the prerecorded videotapes were produced in a unique setting for a unique purpose, they reduce the impact of the Observer's Paradox on the participants.

The prerecorded data also offer a unique benefit resulting from the analysis of student interpreters. Since student interpreters are presumably not fully proficient in the task of interactive interpreting, it is precisely the areas where students have difficulty that could indicate relevant issues in the analysis of real-life interpreted interaction. That is, the analysis of student interpreters can benefit not only interpreting pedagogy, but also can provide useful insights regarding aspects of the task so often overlooked or taken for granted by skilled professionals.

The student interpreters in the prerecorded data were engaged in the real task of interpreting. They were providing access to an interaction between two interlocutors who had been invited to attend a day of class in order to interact with someone not using their native language. Because the invited participants do not know both languages fluently (or at least do not have access to them), the student interpreters were actually engaged in the task of interpreting the interaction between the two languages. Nevertheless, it cannot be denied that classroom role play differs from real-life interaction. In the case of a medical interview, the stakes of participants who are playing the roles of doctor and patient do not necessarily reflect the concerns of patients and doctors in real-life medical encounters.

Data Selection

In an effort to capitalize on the benefits and to reduce the limitations of each of the types of data collected for this study, two cases were selected for analysis and comparison. One case consists of a prerecorded role play of a medical interview as interpreted by an interpreting student. The second case consists of a professional interpreter interpreting a real-life medical interview in a pediatric setting. The examination and comparison of these two cases provides useful information regarding the influences interpreters have on inter-preted interactions. In addition, examination of these two cases pro-vides useful information regarding the application of role plays in in-terpreter education.

Case 1: Mock Medical Interview

The mock medical interview took place in a fairly large classroom where interpreting is taught. Video cameras and related equipment are available and used in this room on a daily basis. The mock med-ical interview lasted for 7.16 minutes. The interview included three participants who were essentially facing one another, although the interpreter was seated more to one side of the "doctor," who was across from the Deaf "patient" (see figure 2.1). The participants re-mained seated throughout the encounter. The instructor and other students were present and observing the interaction as a part of the class but were not visible on the videotape and did not interact with the visible participants.

All three participants were white and middle-class; two were hearing women, and one was a Deaf man. One of the hearing women was an interpreting student in the class. She was in her early to mid-twenties and was the designated interpreter for the mock encounter. The other hearing woman was also interested in interpreting, and al-though she was not a student in the class, she was invited to partic-ipate in the role play of a medical encounter. She was in her early fifties and played the part of the doctor. English was the first lan-guage of both hearing women, and both were studying ASL as a sec-ond language. The Deaf man, who was in his late thirties, was a na-tive signer who attended residential schools and who often taught ASL as a second language.[1] He primarily signed ASL throughout the encounter.

X Doctor

Patient X   *X Interpreter*

Figure 2.1. Mock Interview: Logistics

Case 2: Actual Medical Interview

The actual medical interview took place in a pediatrician's office in a suburban, middle-class neighborhood. The encounter lasted for 26.31 minutes. A total of six people participated in this encounter: the doctor, the nurse, the interpreter, the mother, the child, and the researcher. The examination room was quite small and, as a result, no more than four participants were visible at a time on the recording. The researcher and camera were situated just inside the door (almost behind the open door, in fact) and very close to the wall. As the researcher faced the room, a weight scale was located to her right against the same wall. This wall intersected with the back wall, which had windows leading to the outside of the building. This back wall was directly across from the wall housing the door to the examining room. An examining table was located along the wall across from the camera. Against the front wall, between the end of the examining table and the door, was a counter with papers on it, used by the doctor and nurse to make notes. Although the participants frequently moved around within the room, for much of the interview the mother faced the camera, with the interpreter located to her left (see figure 2.2). The interpreter was facing the doctor (who was to the mother's right). The child was either being examined or in his mother's arms.

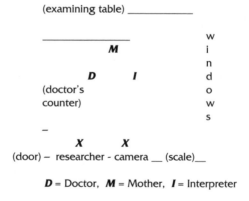

Figure 2.2. Actual Interview: Logistics

All six participants were white and middle class. The doctor was a hearing male in his mid- to upper fifties. The nurse was a hearing female in her late thirties to early forties. Both medical practitioners were native speakers of English and did not know ASL. Although the doctor indicated that he has cared for other deaf patients, he had not worked with an interpreter before, and indicated prior to this interview that he normally communicated with deaf patients by writing notes back and forth. The researcher was a hearing female in her early thirties who was a native speaker of English and who learned ASL as a second language. She was also a professional, certified ASL-English interpreter. The interpreter in the actual medical interview was a hearing female in her mid-thirties. She was bilingual in both ASL and English and had Deaf parents who were fluent ASL signers. She also has had extensive experience as an interpreter educator. The mother, a Deaf native signer of ASL, was almost thirty. She attended residential schools and taught ASL as an adult. Her son was hearing and was about eighteen months old. The mother was approximately five months pregnant with her second child.

Two Cases Compared

Two aspects of the cases under examination are worth noting here. First, based on the aspects of contact signing identified by Lucas and Valli (1992), the mother in the actual medical interview primarily used a contact variety of signing in her discourse. This could be due to a number of factors, many of which have already been discussed. An additional reason for her signing choice could be that she is holding her son for much of the interview. Thus, one hand is not available for communication, and so she uses a lot of fingerspelling and other one-handed signs. Since language choices are often unconscious, it is impossible to know for certain why she chose a contact variety of signing. Nevertheless, her language choice influenced the signing of the interpreter, who incorporated contact signing into many of her renditions in the examples that follow. Unlike the Deaf participant in the actual medical interview, the Deaf participant in the mock interview primarily signed ASL. He had no reason to sign one-handed (and he does not do so), and he was not in an actual medical office or faced with the presence of a researcher. Whatever the reasons for their language choices, it is worth noting that there was a difference in language use by participants in the two encounters.

A second issue worth noting has to do with the length of the encounters. As stated earlier, the actual medical interview lasted for 26.31 minutes. It is interesting to note that the actual medical interview, in which the medical practitioners have the time constraints often cited in literature regarding problems in medical discourse, is almost four times longer than the mock interview occurring in a classroom. One might expect that a mock interview would be the encounter that is not constrained by time. One possible reason for the time differential is that the participants in the mock interview simply ran out of fabricated material. A second possibility is that the teacher ended the interview for pedagogical purposes. It is also possible that the doctor in the actual medical interview extended the encounter as a result of the presence of the researcher and camera. Similarly, the doctor might have extended the interview because of the presence of the interpreter. The mother mentioned after the interview concluded that it had lasted longer than normal. If it was the presence of the interpreter that caused this change in behavior, it is worth investigating whether extended length of time is a feature of interpreted medical interviews. However, if it was the presence of the researcher that caused the time extension, it is worth pursuing other avenues for collecting more realistic examples of how doctors interact with deaf patients via interpreters under normal time constraints.

Analysis of Two Interpreted Interviews

One of the difficulties in collecting data from real-life interpreted medical encounters involves technological challenges. For example, in order to interpret between ASL and English, interpreters must be positioned so that they can both see, and be seen by, any Deaf consumers. Yet, analysis requires that both the Deaf participants' and the interpreter's signing be accessible to the camera view. Bringing additional cameras into an interview setting is not only increasingly intrusive, but challenging to coordinate for later viewing. Thus, one advantage of the prerecorded mock medical interview data used here is the relatively unobtrusive presence of multiple cameras in the classroom environment. Another is the availability of advanced technology to make all parties visible on the screen. Because intrusiveness is significantly less of an issue in the mock medical encounter, the advantages of advanced technology can be used to obtain data that offers access and insights potentially unavailable in the actual interpreted medical encounter. Nevertheless, it cannot be denied that while simulating a medical interview, the mock interview will clearly differ from medical encounters that occur in the real-world context of hospitals and clinics.

As anticipated, analysis of the actual medical interview did exhibit evidence of the influence of camera and researcher presence. For example, at times during the pediatric interview the mother and child can be seen waving to the camera. In fact, the mother refers to the camera and researcher in an apparent attempt to distract the child from crying. In addition, the doctor, who essentially ignores the camera and researcher throughout the interview, makes a comment as he leaves the office indicating his awareness of their presence. Finally, the interpreter, who occasionally gazes in the direction of the camera (for example, in response to the mother and child waving), commented after the interview session that she had been tempted once to ask the researcher (also a certified professional interpreter) for assistance with the interpreting task. Thus, all informants were affected by the presence of camera and researcher/interpreter, unlike the role play, which was videotaped as a routine part of class and prior to any consideration of submission for research purposes. Nevertheless, the actual interview offers authenticity in the medical setting that the role play does not. Hopefully, through a comparison of these two encounters, both authenticity and naturalness will be represented in the data, and the impact of the Observer's Paradox, to some extent, will be minimized.

Transcription Issues
Transcription of signed language data is never easy. Part of the difficulty arises from a lack of standardization. Winston and Ball indicate

that the need to include visual and spatial information, and the need for consistency in the use of transcription symbols, are among the concerns to be addressed in the process of standardization (Winston and Ball, 1994). Because ASL is not a written language and, perhaps even more important, because of the existence of multiple articulators (including fingers, hands, arms, shoulders, neck, head, mouth, cheeks, eyes, and eyebrows), written transcription can lose more of the original than it captures.

Mischler (1991) compares transcription to photography, indicating that "what we assume to have been 'really' there, and how the photographer selected and framed the event, and how the photograph is presented and located within the flow of other information . . . all influence our understanding." A transcription reflects and emphasizes what the transcriber thinks is relevant within the data. Perhaps for this reason, Ochs (1979) suggests that transcripts should be based on theoretical goals. Because the focus here is to analyze the interpreters' utterances as they interact with the discourse as a whole, a musical-score format of transcription is used.

The musical-score format of transcription is one way of representing the simultaneous and overlapping nature of interactive discourse. As described by Ehlich (1993), the musical-score format allows the sequence of events to unfold from left to right on a horizontal line, while the list of participants occurring from top to bottom allows each person's utterances to be captured within a single moment of overlap. For example, in figure 2.3, an excerpt of the transcript from the actual medical interview illustrates the musical-score format. In this example, the first event in the time line (from left to right) is that of the doctor entering the examining room. Upon

Figure 2.3. Sample of musical-score transcription.

his entry he says, "Hello." Overlapping with the latter part of this brief utterance, the interpreter initiates her ASL rendition, indicated with the English gloss HELLO (see Transcription Conventions in Appendix 2 for information regarding the use of glosses and other transcription features). Just after the interpreter signs HELLO, the mother signs, HELLO. Once again, during the latter part of her utterance, the interpreter begins her English rendition of this when she says, "Hi." Throughout this exchange, the child is silent. This example illustrates that the musical-score format not only indicates the occurrence of these four utterances, but also, at least roughly, their relationship to one another in time.

The musical-score format is particularly useful for an interpreted encounter. Since most of what is uttered by noninterpreter participants (i.e., the doctor, nurse, and mother) is reuttered by the interpreter, there is a tremendous amount of overlap throughout the data. Moreover, because the interpreter not only uses two languages but two modalities as well, it is possible that she will produce utterances in more than one modality at a time (both signing and speaking). In order to accurately and unambiguously represent the interpreter's utterances, two lines of transcription are ascribed to the interpreter throughout the data analyzed: one for English utterances and the other for ASL utterances (as marked in figure 2.3).

Two additional points are relevant with regard to the transcription format. First, because this is a preliminary study of the influence of one participant in deference to her social role (interpreter), the transcript identifies all of the participants on the basis of their social roles within the medical interview context (e.g., doctor, mother, interpreter, and so forth). This practice is not intended to dehumanize the participants, nor is it intended to suggest that a single social role can capture the identity of any given individual. In fact, as Schiffrin (1993) points out, social identities are situated within activities and are dynamic, not static, in nature.

Second, although there is no researcher present during the mock interview, the researcher is present throughout the actual medical interview. The main task of the researcher is to operate the video camera, and thus, she is not visible on the screen. Because all of her utterances are in ASL, they are not accessible for transcription purposes. Moreover, the participants rarely address or respond to the researcher during the course of the medical interview. Therefore, no line of the transcript is provided for the researcher as one of the potential interlocutors. This is not intended to hide her presence, however, and all of her audible contributions (such as laughter) are indicated within the appropriate line.

Although the musical-score format allows for the indication of discourse phenomenon such as pausing (by leaving appropriate portions of the line blank), certain transcription conventions related to both spoken and signed language transcription are adhered to within the transcript. (For details regarding the transcription of both the ASL and English discourse, see Transcription Conventions in Appendix 2.) However, as Locker McKee (1992) points out regarding indication of some aspects of ASL, transcription can provide an etic or an emic description of the signs. She describes etic transcriptions as those that focus on the form of the sign, and emic transcriptions as those that emphasize the meaning of a given sign. The transcription for this study uses some etic features (such as INDEX [rt] for a point to the right) and some emic (PRO.3 [baby]) to indicate the meaning of a pronoun rather than simply the form, depending on the issue being discussed. In addition, nonmanual and contextual information is included where necessary to enhance readability of the transcript.

Translations of the ASL are provided where necessary to make the transcript more accessible. In addition, when specific parts of an example are particularly relevant, the relevant portion of the transcript is either provided in isolation or highlighted in bold within the transcribed example. The transcript was originally produced by the researcher, with assistance from both native signers and qualified interpreters (both hearing and Deaf) to promote accuracy.

The transcription of discourse in any language involves consideration of a variety of theoretical issues. However, the problems facing signed language transcription are even greater than those faced by spoken language linguists, as a result of both the unwritten status of signed languages and their articulatory complexities. Nevertheless, an attempt has been made to address these theoretical issues, especially as they interact within multiparty, bilingual, interpreted discourse.

Examining Interpreted Medical Interviews

The Interpreter's Paradox exists because interpreters are faced with the goal of providing access to interaction of which they are not a part, while they are, in fact, physically and interactionally present. In order to examine the interpreter's involvement in interpreted encounters, it is first necessary to understand the nature of such encounters as they occur without the presence of interpreters. Thus, this chapter has provided a discussion of medical interview discourse as well as a discussion of findings regarding the influence of interpreters in such settings. Because the collection of ASL-English interpreted medical interviews is challenging for both humanistic and technological reasons, the focus here will be on the analysis and comparison of two cases of interpreted encounters: a mock medical interview interpreted by a student and an actual medical interview interpreted by a native bilingual, certified professional. Theoretical issues regarding the transcription of both spoken and signed languages, with an emphasis on the issue of interpreted encounters, provides the rationale for the use of a musical-score format of transcription.

Analysis of the data is based on consideration of a variety of factors including identification of the originator of each utterance and whether or not that utterance was accessible to other participants, identification of the addressee on the basis of linguistic or paralinguistic cues, and documentation of turn-sequences, false starts, repairs, occurrences of constructed dialogue, use of question forms, reference, and so forth. Needless to say, the data reflect the complexity of interpreted discourse. As a data-driven study, the relevant features of the discourse have become clear through examination of the problem at hand: what is the interpreter's influence on the interactive discourse?

3

Interactive Frames
and Schema
in Interpreted
Medical Encounters

RESEARCH REGARDING interactive discourse is a complicated undertaking. When interaction between two or more monolingual parties is facilitated by an interpreter, the potential complexities of the interaction are compounded. Are interpreters expected to relay utterances as if they were easily transferable from the linguistic structure and culturally embedded significance of one language and speaker to that of another? Schiffrin (1993) identifies at least two ways of framing the act of speaking for another, as motivated by friendship and support for the second party, or as motivated by more self-centered concerns. This suggests the possibility that interpreters, whose function it is to "speak" for others, could frame the task in ways that impact the nature of an interaction.

Part of the complexity of examining an interpreted encounter is that the interpreter might bring one frame to the event, while the primary participants bring others. Moreover, each participant, including the interpreter, comes to the interaction with a unique set of experiences and background information. Research regarding the interaction between frames and knowledge schema in interactive discourse (Tannen and Wallat 1983, 1987; Hoyle 1993; Schiffrin 1993; Smith 1993) indicates that participants' frames can overlap, and knowledge schemas can be mismatched within a single event.

Frames and Schema in Discourse

In order to examine the interaction between frames and schema in interpreted discourse, it is first necessary to distinguish the meaning of these terms. The terms *frame* and *schema* and even the term *script* have been applied to the study of interaction by scholars from numerous fields, including psychology, sociology, anthropology, linguistics, and artificial intelligence. As a result, these terms have received diverse and detailed attention. For some researchers, the three terms are essentially synonymous. For others, they are not.

Bateson (1955, 1972) discusses the ways in which activity is framed by participants. In particular, he discusses the fact that a behavior, such as fighting, can be signaled and interpreted as playful rather than serious. This use of the term *frame* as the way in which interaction can be understood is consistent with Goffman's analysis of frames (1974). Goffman defines frames as "definitions of a situation [which] are built up in accordance with principles of organization which govern events—at least social ones—and our subjective involvement in them" (11). Goffman discusses an activity, such as fighting, that can be framed by an outer rim, either consistent with the inner activity yielding a primary framework, or transforming the event into a different activity, as in the case of play fighting. Goffman discusses many aspects of frames, including various layers of frames, transformations or keyings, frame breaks, and misframing. In addition, Goffman (1981) expands on his analysis of frames, discussing various potential roles held by the participants in an interaction.

Minsky (1975) provides a detailed description of frames, which he defines as "remembered frameworks to be adapted to fit reality" (212). In his discussion of memory and stereotypes of situations, Minsky, like Kuipers (1975), emphasizes the concept of frames as knowledge structures. In fact, he suggests that his definition of frame is similar to Bartlett's notion of schema (1932). Gumperz also seems to compare the terms *frame* and *schema*, as well as the term *script*, suggesting that all three terms essentially refer to ways in which participants apply world knowledge in order to understand social encounters (1982, 154).

Language provides evidence regarding the way an individual frames an event. Fillmore discusses linguistic frames at the morphemic level, giving an example of a "commercial transaction." In his example, he describes the various ways in which the transaction can be framed as if there were a camera view of the transaction, emphasizing certain participant perspectives (i.e., merchant's view versus customer's view) through the use of such terms as *buy, sell, pay, money, merchant,* and *customer* (1976, 13). For instance, to *buy* a car and to *sell* a car are two different ways of framing the transaction. Chafe discusses frames in a similar manner, suggesting that frames focus on the individual(s) in an event (i.e., via agent, patient, beneficiary) (1977). As will be seen shortly, both Fillmore and Chafe make a further distinction between the terms *frame* and *schema.*

Tannen (1979) and Tannen and Wallat (1983, 1987, 1993) also provide definitions for the term *frame.* Tannen, who discusses various applications of the terms *frame, schema,* and *script,* considers frames to be structures of expectations. In Tannen and Wallat, interactive frames are defined as "a sense of what activity is being engaged in" (1987, 207). The term "knowledge schema" is used to refer to "participants' expectations about people, objects, events and settings in the world." Tannen and Wallat seem to suggest that both interactive frames and knowledge schema are dynamic structures of expectations. In more recent work, some have adopted Tannen and Wallat's notions, while others cite Goffman's definitions.

Despite some apparent overlaps in conceptions of frame and schema, the term *schema* has a different history from the term *frame.* The first reference to *schema* as a concept of dynamic knowledge structures that function as "active developing patterns" in an individual's memory is generally attributed to Bartlett (1932). Bartlett defines *schema* as "an active organization of past reactions, or of past experiences, which must always be supposed to be operating in any well-adapted organic response" (201). Bartlett emphasizes the dynamic nature of these knowledge structures, although as Tannen (1979) points out, not all who followed him have perpetuated that dynamic nature.

Minsky (1975) and Gumperz (1982) seem to see the terms as essentially the same. However, for Fillmore (1976), frames and schema appear to be distinguishable. He suggests that frames activate certain schema. For example, in the sentence "He was on land briefly this afternoon," the phrase "on land" is described as being part of a frame that implies a counterpart "at sea." Thus, this frame activates a schema of a "sea voyage" (15). Chafe (1977) also separates the notions of frames and schema. He provides an example of the "bureaucratic runaround" as a schema that includes a purpose, a series of deflections, and a resolution often at odds with the original purpose (43). For both Fillmore and Chafe, the notion of schema includes knowledge that represents a temporal ordering of events.

The concept of temporal order as a knowledge structure has been referred to in the literature by yet another label, *script.* The term *script* is attributed primarily to the work of Schank and Abelson (1977), who not only provide a detailed description of scripts but also other knowledge structures, including plans and goals. Schank and Abelson define script as a "standard event sequence" (38). Three types of scripts that they discuss are situational scripts, personal scripts, and instrumental scripts. Each type of script might contain different parts. For example, a situational script can include a track, various roles, entry conditions, and scene sequences. A well-known example of a situational script is the restaurant script. The track in a restaurant script would refer to the type of restaurant, such as a coffee shop or a cafeteria. The roles might include customer, waiter, cashier, owner, and so forth. The entry conditions that are relevant in a restaurant script include the likelihood that the customer is hungry and has money with which to purchase food. Since a script can be seen as a sequence of scenes in which one or more events are likely to transpire, the restaurant script includes the following scenes:

Scene 1. Entering

Scene 2. Ordering

Scene 3. Eating

Scene 4. Exiting

The exiting scene could include such activities as paying the bill and leaving a tip. The scenes are not restricted to a single occurrence. For example, after scene 3, the customer could return to scene 2 by ordering additional food.

Evidence of the existence of the restaurant script can be seen in the following example:

> John went to a restaurant. He asked the waitress for a coq au vin. He paid the check and left. (Schank and Abelson 1977, 38)

The use of the definite and explicit referent "the waitress" might be surprising since there is no prior mention of her in the discourse. Schank and Abelson suggest that the earlier reference to "a restaurant" is enough to evoke a restaurant script, in which "waitress" is an expected role. Thus, the use of the definite, explicit referring term is evidence of the existence of the conceptual structure of a restaurant script.

Script, then, appears to exist as one type of knowledge structure. This is true not only of situational scripts, as described above, but also of personal and instrumental scripts. Schank and Abelson describe personal scripts as the sequence of events based on what is in the mind of one participant. For instance, "John" in the preceding example might follow a script resulting from his interest in getting to know the waitress (1977, 62). Since this interest is only truly knowable by John, this is an example of a personal script. Instrumental scripts are those in which a participant engages in a rigid sequence of activities, such as lighting a cigarette or frying an egg (65). While scripts focus on sequences of events, other information, such as props and roles within an event, are also part of the conceptual structure. Several scholars, including Bobrow and Norman (1975), Fillmore (1976), and Chafe (1977), have referred to sequential knowledge as at least one aspect of schematic structures. Thus, it seems likely that scripts could be considered to be one type of knowledge structure, or schema. In addition, Bobrow and Norman suggest that schematic descriptions can include measuring operations and spatial representations.

Recurring Constructs

Regardless of the terminology used to describe them, the constructs addressed in most of the literature on frames, schemas, and scripts can be described as two basic concepts: perspectives and knowledge structures. Perspectives have been discussed as they apply to both activities and participants. Knowledge structures refer to conceptual information such as where an event occurs and how it unfolds. Although these two concepts are distinguishable from one another, the relationship between the two appears to be quite complex.

The term *perspective* is used here to represent varying points of view. This term seems to be comparable to a construct that is at least a part of most definitions of the term *frame*. Despite the fact that some broad definitions of *frame* might include reference to conceptual knowledge, the term *perspective* specifically refers to the way in which events or participants are viewed.

Perspectives on an event can be multilayered. A good example of the ways that perspectives can frame events is Goffman's discussion of inner and outer layers (1974). What Goffman refers to as framing an activity is that aspect that allows individuals to perceive fighting as either serious or playful. Regarding participants, there are potentially many different perspectives. For example, Schank and Abelson (1977) discuss the various roles involved in a restaurant script, pointing out that a perspective encompassing all roles is a whole view, whereas other perspectives might represent specifically the view of a customer, a waitress, and so forth. Thus, it is possible to examine an event from either a situational perspective or from the perspective of participants.

Unlike the notion of perspectives, knowledge structures refer specifically to the conceptual information available to an individual. In keeping with most of the work on schema, knowledge structures are dynamic and develop on the basis of experiential input. Structures of knowledge could conceivably take many forms. For example, some of the types of structures addressed in the literature reviewed here include information about settings, objects or props, participants, and sequences of events. This definition is fairly consistent with that in Tannen and Wallat (1987), and shares features with other work, including Goffman (1974), Fillmore (1976), Chafe (1977), and Schank and Abelson (1977).

Although distinguishing the two constructs, *perspectives* and *knowledge structures*, can be useful, the problem of how they relate to one another appears to be complex. Three possible relationships include knowledge structures (hereafter referred to as schema) as primary, perspectives (hereafter referred to as frames) as primary, or some type of dynamic interaction between the two as of primary importance. That is, if schema consists of multiple interrelated information that includes participants, props, and so forth, it is conceivable that every schema has a multitude of potential frames from which to approach a given situation. For example, in the schema of a restaurant script, one could take the whole view or the view of any one of the participants. Conversely, if framing an event is crucial to understanding interaction, perhaps every frame is supported by relevant schema. In this case, the frame is of primary relevance, and would activate the appropriate schema. A third possibility is that both of the previous conceptions are true. In other words, every frame might be supported by relevant schema at the same time that every schema includes a multitude of potentially relevant frames. If this is the case, it would seem that every interaction consists of a dynamic and continuous negotiation of relevant frames and schema, each of which reflects and contributes to the presence of the other. Though complicated, the interactive view seems to make sense intuitively and could explain why these concepts have received mixed and overlapping discussion in the past.

An attempt has been made here to clarify the constructs underlying the use of the terms *frame* and *schema*. Despite overlaps in conceptualizations of these constructs as applied to the terms, two basic concepts are identifiable—knowledge structures and perspectives. In order to avoid confusion by delineating new terms to refer to these concepts, in this study, the term *schema* refers to knowledge structures, conceptions of people, events, and so forth. *Frames* will refer to perspectives, which can be a particular view of an event or of participants. This distinction between frames and schema should be identifiable on the basis of linguistic evidence. For instance, with regard to the example of a restaurant script discussed earlier, reference to "the waitress" evokes at least one interrelated schema and frame. The use of this reference evokes a schema (the knowledge structure), relating to restaurants; the people (waitresses and waiters, customers, cooks), the events (entering, ordering, eating), and so forth. At the same time, use of the term "the waitress" also evokes a particular frame (particular view of the events or participants); the perception of the restaurant is that of a "sit down" place of business rather than a cafeteria. Once this frame has been evoked, the relevant schema immediately come into play, identifying the relevant events, participants, and so on to this frame (such as menus, for example).

An analogy from the stage can help to demonstrate the distinction, as well as the interrelationship of these terms. In a particular scene in a theatrical script, a director can frame the scene in any one of numerous ways by providing signals that evoke the desired schema from the audience. For instance, if the scene consists of a female and male actor involved in a discussion, the words in the scene could be framed as either suspicious and dangerous, or romantic and happy by using dark or bright lights, and low-pitched, slow music versus light, up-tempo music. The use of particular lighting and music causes the audience to retrieve certain schema related to the appropriate frame. Conversely, on the basis of their schema, the interaction will be framed in one way or the other. The audience is likely to develop expectations regarding the sequence of events about to unfold, as well as each character's role within them, on the basis of the interaction between their frames and schema. This distinction between the terms is the one that will be applied to interpreted interactions.

Frames and Schema in Interpreted Interaction: Mock Medical Encounter

The interpreted role play of a medical encounter can be analyzed in terms of the framing of the activity, and the evidence of the schema underlying the frames. Evidence from the role play suggests that the layers of framed activity include at least three laminations of the inner activity: interpreting. Interpreting is seen as the most central activity, because without it the speech event would likely not continue. In addition, the purpose of the activity is for the student to interpret. Despite the fact that this is a mock encounter, the student truly is interpreting, since the Deaf and hearing interlocutors are depending on her in order to communicate their parts in the role play.

The next layer of activity is the medical encounter, and most of the discourse includes medical discussion and treatment options. The medical encounter is transformed by the third layer, the role play. Goffman (1974, 58–59) describes these types of keying as technical redoings, being engaged in for the purpose of skills development. Finally, the outermost layer is "a class." This layer is primarily evident through the bracketing at the beginning or end of the role play, and will not be discussed here. Nevertheless, it is important to recognize the existence of all the layers in order to analyze the interaction between these frames and their underlying schema (see figure 3.1). The data suggest that each participant shares these frames for the activity at hand. However, there is also evidence that the participants do not always share the same schema for these frames.

Role-Play Frame

There is very little evidence of the role-play frame in the mock medical interview. There are no explicit references to the fact that this is a practice event. Possibly the only evidence suggesting that this is not an actual medical event is found in the doctor's slowed prosody and false starts when responding to a medical question for which she does not necessarily have the technical knowledge.

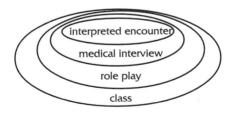

Figure 3.1. Frames within mock medical encounter.

In example 3.1, the patient has just asked the doctor to explain what an ulcer is. Lines 10–11 include part of the doctor's response:

Example 3.1

10

Doctor: What's happening is, in your stomach?

11

The, uh, digestive enzymes actually attack . . . the di— the— . . . the lining.

Although it is possible that a real medical doctor would hesitate when explaining a medical concept in lay terms, presumably the woman playing the doctor does not have medical training. Thus, the hesitation, false starts, and repairs suggest that she is "ad-libbing" in the role-play frame, as though searching for an answer to the question.

The woman playing the role of the doctor could have responded in many ways. If she did not possess the information necessary to respond appropriately, she could have said so, which would break the medical interview frame since most doctors would have this information. In addition, she could have referred the patient to another source, which might also represent unusual behavior on the part of a doctor. She also might have used an explicit frame bracket to temporarily exit the role-play frame (Hoyle 1993). For instance, she might have said, "Time out. I can't really answer that question." However, the fact that she responds as she does suggests that she prefers to be consistent within the role-play frame and does not want to break it. The doctor's response in example 3.1 also provides some information about the schema she brings to this frame. She apparently has a schema regarding the appropriate response from a doctor (perhaps a medical interview script).

It is interesting to note that the slowed prosody, pauses, and self-repairs in the preceding example are the only evidence of the role-play frame. All of the participants appear to take the exercise very seriously. Whether or not their serious treatment of the role play allows them to successfully replicate an actual medical encounter remains to be seen, however. It would be interesting to study the effectiveness of role playing as a training strategy for interpreters.

Medical Interview Frame

That the encounter has been framed as a medical interview is evident through certain linguistic signals that are relevant to the appropriate schema. It is not clear whether the medical interview frame activates the relevant schema, whether the schematic signals activate the medical interview frame, or some other interaction between the two. Nevertheless, the occurrence of the features discussed here indicates that the encounter has been framed as a medical interview. Because there are no interruptions or other conflicts in the discourse, the participants seem to share similar schema as well. This schema includes, for one thing, a medical interview script, consisting of at least some of these basic scenes:

1. Opening

2. Medical history

3. Examination

4. Diagnosis

5. Consultation

6. Medical advice

Scenes 1, 4, 5, and 6 occur in the role play. The medical interview is considered to be a recheck after a prior visit approximately one week before. Therefore, scenes 2 and 3 are not included in the data, although reference is made to an "upper GI" test supposedly performed at an earlier date.

The unfolding of this script, as well as the topics and question-answer sequences within the interview, provides evidence of the medical interview frame. The doctor initiates the opening of the medical interview by the doctor asking the patient about his current state of health:

Example 3.2

3

    Doctor: And how are you feeling this morning?

After a brief response to this information-seeking question, the doctor presents a diagnosis on the basis of previous test results in lines 6 and 7 below:

Example 3.3*

6

P:

D: **Well your test y'know, you remember, the =**

I: = but the medicine has helped a little.

I: YOUR =

7

P: PRO.1 NERVOUS PRO.1 =

D:= **upper GI that you had last week...did show that you have an ulcer, so, th- there is a problem.**

I:

I: =   TEST   PRO.1   REMEMBER   TEST   LAST-WEEK?   U-L-C-E-R   G-I

8

P: = PRO.1 NERVOUS PRO.1

D:

I: yeah, I'm nervous.

I: PRO.1 PROBLEM ANSW- RESPONSE SAY =

9

P: HAVE? HAVE? U-C-L (pause) **WHAT U-L-C?**

D:

I: Oh, I have I have an ulcer? Um, what's that exactly?

I: = WHAT? HAVE U-L-C-E-R HAVE.

---

*In this example, and most of the examples from the mock interview, the following abbreviations will be used: P = patient, D = doctor, N = nurse, I = interpreter.

The deaf patient responds to this with a request for information about ulcers in line 9. By doing so, he has indicated that the doctor has medical information that he does not. This moves the interview out of the diagnosis phase and into a consultation phase, in which the doctor and patient discuss the meaning of the diagnosis. The doctor then moves into the advice stage of the interview by recommending a dietary change:

Example 3.4

25

D: Uh, I do have a list of, uh, food that I'd like you to . . . try to stick to

---

The doctor subsequently describes the recommended dietary changes for the patient. At one point during the encounter a woman's voice requests that the doctor tend to an emergency. Thus, the mock medical interview even incorporates a "Waiting for the Doctor" scene likely to occur in a medical interview script.

Evidence of the medical interview frame includes topics, question-and-answer sequences, and the unfolding script of events. The mock medical interview itself appears to run relatively smoothly. This seems to suggest that all the participants frame this encounter as a medical interview, and share schema similar enough to support that frame with limited repair or renegotiation. One reason for this could be the commonality of medical interviews. Most people living in the United States are likely to share some semblance of a medical interview script. The fact that all three participants have access to this similar schema would conceivably contribute to the smooth nature of the interaction. Another potential explanation for this could be the fact that neither the doctor nor the patient have a real-life vested interest in the medical part of the encounter. So far, it appears that the role-play frame and the medical interview frame are based on schema shared by the participants. However, both of these frames are outer layers of the activity at hand. Because the innermost activity appears to be the interpreted encounter itself, it is interesting to note some mismatches that occur within the interpreted encounter frame.

Interpreted Encounter Frame

Analysis of the data indicates that all three participants share an interpreted encounter frame; that is, all three participants frame this interaction as an interpreted one. However, each participant seems to have a different schema regarding interpreted encounters. Examples of the mismatch between schemas are discussed below.

Evidence that all three participants frame this event as an interpreted encounter can be seen in example 3.5. This example occurs at the beginning of the interaction, just prior to the initiation of the medical interview itself. All three participants are already seated when the interpreter introduces herself:

Example 3.5

1

P:

D: Oh, you're the interpreter for today.

I: . . . and I'm gonna be the sign lang- language interpreter for today.

I: . . . POSS.1 SIGN LANGUAGE INTERPRETER LANGUAGE NOW. PRO.1, PRO.3, PRO.1 OH INTERPRETER=
     I'll be the sign language interpreter- language for today. I- she said, "Oh, I'll be the =

2

P: (nods)

D: It's nice to meet you.

I: Thank you, it's nice to meet you too.

I: NOW PRO.1, #OK #OK. PRO.1- NICE TO MEET PRO.1 THANKS NICE MEET-TO (doctor) SAME.
       interpreter for today, oh okay." It's nice to meet me. Thanks, it's nice to meet you, too.

In this segment the interpreter introduces herself, and the doctor acknowledges her presence by repeating, "Oh, you're the interpreter for today." The interpreter has chosen to simultaneously sign and speak her initial utterance, and she interprets the doctor's response. At that point, the patient nods, apparently affirming or agreeing with the recent propositions.

Although all three participants seem to frame this as an interpreted event, there is evidence that each has a different schema regarding the interpreter's role within that event. The doctor appears to view the interpreter as a third participant who is a professional expert. This can be seen from the doctor's utterances that are directed at the interpreter, including those in lines 1–2 above in which the doctor acknowledges and greets the interpreter as one might greet a colleague. Evidence that the doctor sees the interpreter as a professional expert can be seen in line 22 below, in which the doctor interrupts her explanation to the patient, turns to look at the interpreter, and asks her how to sign something:

Example 3.6

21

D: It's only serious if we put it off and don't treat it,

22

and just ignore the problem . . . (gaze shift to interpreter) what is— is there a sign for ulcer?

This particular word, *ulcer*, has already been the topic of the discourse for some time. Hence, it does not appear that the doctor is asking this question as a part of the doctor-patient interaction per se. It is possible that the woman asks this question "in the character" of the doctor. It is also possible that she is simply curious for her own personal reasons, having nothing to do with the role play per se. The doctor could also be asking as a move to include the interpreter, who has not participated for some time. Nevertheless, the fact that the doctor requests this information from the interpreter rather than the patient (who is a native signer) suggests that her conceptualization of the interpreter is as a professional expert who can provide the information in response to her question. Even if the woman believes that the Deaf patient is equally capable of answering the question, but, perhaps, feels that asking the interpreter removes one step from the process and saves time, she is still treating the interpreter as an expert capable of supplying the information.

The interpreter's schema regarding her role as an interpreter appears to differ, however. The interpreter seems to view her role as a service provider who would prefer not to be involved in the doctor-patient dyadic interaction. For example, when the doctor speaks to the interpreter directly, attempting to ratify her as an addressee, she rejects the attempt. This can be seen in example 3.7 below, in her response to the doctor's question:

Example 3.7

22

P:

D: What is- is there a sign for ulcer?

I:

I: **PRO.3   PRO.1   SIGN =**
                                            She asked me, "What's your sign

23

P: (hand flip)
                                      (*Whatever.*)

D: **No, huh?   Oh, okay =**

I: Umm . . .

I: FOR **U-L-C-E-R** PRO.2?...ASK-TO (interpreter) QUESTION.   NO SIGN? ASK TO (interpreter)
   for ulcer."   *She asked me a question.*   *There isn't one! She asked me.*

24

P: UM, PRO.1 UH U-L-C-E-R
          Um, I just spell it.

D: = **Well, at any rate, um I do have a- I have a list of-**   Oh, okay.

I:

I: Um, yeah, you can just fingerspell it.   #OH #OK #OK

```
25
P:
D: Uh, I do have a list of uh, food that I'd like you to . . . try to stick to—
I:
I:                                                       HAVE LIST FOOD RIGHT =
```

Although the doctor has directly addressed the interpreter, who does, in fact, know the answer to the question, the interpreter does not comply with the request for information until she successfully elicits it from the patient. The interpreter's and the patient's utterances in line 23 occur only in ASL, and during this period of silence there is an empty slot in the question-answer pair that occurred in the English dialogue (Schegloff and Sacks 1973). The doctor attempts to fill the slot in line 23, but, with no compliance from the interpreter, resumes the interview frame in lines 23–24, introducing a list of food for the patient to eat. While the interpreter has not responded to the doctor, she has not remained "silent" either. Her response to the doctor's question can be seen in lines 22–23; she explains to the patient what has just occurred. Her explanation consists of a statement, rather than a question. The interpreter does not present the first part of an adjacency pair to the Deaf patient. Moreover, the interpreter's explanation does not indicate whether or not she has answered the doctor's question. Consequently, the patient cannot know there is an empty slot in the spoken discourse. Not surprisingly, there is no response from the patient. Because the interpreter persists with this strategy, repeating her statement and not relaying the doctor's return to the interview, it appears that the interpreter's goal is for the patient to respond to the request directed at the interpreter. The interpreter's schema of the interpreter's role seems to reject the notion of interpreter as interacting with the hearing doctor, while allowing some interaction with the Deaf patient. If it is within her schema that the patient should respond to the request, and she is assuming that the patient shares her schema, then her utterance in lines 22–23 makes sense. The explanation would be enough information for the patient to either provide the information or explain to the doctor that she should address such questions to him, and not to the interpreter. The long silences, overlapping talk, and interruption in this segment indicate that the three participants do not share the same expectations at this point in the interpreted encounter.

Although the interpreter appears to be unwilling to accept the role of ratified addressee when initiated by the doctor, it is interesting to note that her responses to the patient's attempts to treat her as a ratified addressee are not quite the same. However, as can be seen in both the previous and the following examples, the interpreter does not actually comply with either of the other participants' requests. This supports the contention that her schema regarding the interpreter's role is different from that of either participant.

The patient's view of the interpreter seems to represent a third schema regarding the interpreter role. The patient seems to view the interpreter as a potential participant and advocate. During the medical interview itself, the patient does not attempt to engage in conversation with the interpreter. However, when the doctor leaves the room, the patient immediately begins a dialogue with the interpreter, requesting advice, checking on information provided by the doctor, and asking the interpreter for assistance. This can be seen in the translation of lines 28–36 below (see appendix 3 for the full transcript of these lines):

Example 3.8

28

P: *Hey, what do you think I should do? She says I have an ulcer but . . .*

29

   I don't believe her. She's just making it up.

30

I: *I think you better talk to her. I really don't know anything about ulcers.*

31

P: *[She's just*

32

making it up. I don't trust her . . . hmm, is an ulcer really what she said it is?]

33

I: *I just don't know much about ulcers, it's better to ask the doctor.*

34

P: *Ask the doctor? I can't ask the doctor. I don't trust her. Ugh, doctors . . . it's so*

35

awkward, no way, I can't ask her. Could you ask her? Could you? Um-

36

I: *I'd be happy to interpret any questions you might have. (Doctor reenters.)*

When the patient asks the interpreter for advice, in line 28, the interpreter responds to the patient, but does not comply with his request and refers him back to the doctor. Similarly, in line 32, the patient asks the interpreter to confirm the accuracy of the doctor's information regarding ulcers. Again, the interpreter does not ignore the patient, but does not comply with his request either, referring him to the doctor. Finally, in line 34, the patient asks the interpreter for assistance in asking the doctor for information. For the third time, the interpreter does not comply. This time she responds by indicating that she would be more than happy to interpret, thus, affirming that she will not comply with the patient's request. In this segment, the interpreter's schema is one of professional service provider, while the patient's schema is that of advocate.

It is interesting to note that a discussion of this situation occurred among the role-play participants immediately following the activity. The teacher of the class indicated that the student interpreter provided the kinds of responses that she was being trained to provide (personal communication). However, the Deaf "patient" was very upset with the interpreter's way of handling his questions. He seemed to feel that he was not being supported by the interpreter. This supports the possibility that he and the interpreter have different schema regarding what kind of "support" an interpreter should provide. Perhaps, if the interpreter could find responses more compatible with a Deaf interlocutor's framing of the interpreted encounter, the conflict could be avoided. It would be interesting, in future research, to determine the effect of various interpreter strategies in such a situation.

That the three participants' perspectives regarding the role of the interpreter differ could indicate one of at least two possibilities. Either the participants do not share the frame "Interpreted Encounter," or the event is framed the same way, but the participants do not share the same schema for that frame. Although it might appear to be difficult to distinguish between these two possibilities, it is relevant in a practical sense; if there is a problem resulting from the differences, and the differences are based on the framing of the event, one need only inform all participants of the appropriate (or at least a common) frame so that the event can proceed. If on the other hand, the problem lies within differing schema, simply explicating the interpreted encounter frame (i.e., "This is an interpreted encounter") will not resolve the underlying problem. Rather, more detailed education and demonstration of interpreted encounters would be necessary to rectify the situation. On the basis of this distinction, this analysis indicates that the participants share the Interpreted Encounter frame, but do not share a common schema.

Frames and Schema in Interpreted Interaction:
Actual Medical Encounter

In the mock medical encounter, both the hearing and Deaf participants have had at least some exposure to, and experience with, interpreted interactions. However, many Deaf and hearing people spend only a fraction of their time, if any, in interpreted encounters. Conversely, interpreters spend most of their professional time in situations with Deaf and hearing people who are in a position to communicate with one another. In the actual medical encounter under examination here, the Deaf person has had experience with interpreters. However, the hearing doctor generally interacts with Deaf patients via paper and pencil: he has had limited experience with interpreted medical interviews. Thus, it is interesting to determine what frames and schema the participants bring to the actual medi-

Figure 3.2. Frames within actual medical encounter.

cal encounter, and how this compares to the frames and schema evident in the mock medical encounter. Unlike the student interpreter, the professional interpreter under examination here is performing in a situation involving an actual doctor and nurse (both hearing) as well as a Deaf mother with her sick, hearing baby.

Evidence from the actual medical encounter suggests that the central activity here is the medical interview. Although the presence of the interpreter has a profound impact on the nature of the interaction, if no interpreter were available, the doctor and patient would likely have found an alternative means of communication. The doctor indicated that he had rarely worked with interpreters and that he typically communicated via paper and pencil with Deaf or hard of hearing patients.

At least three laminations of the medical interview are identifiable. First, the medical interview is framed as a pediatric examination. The pediatric examination is framed as an interpreted encounter. The outermost layer of activity is the research study. The four layers of activity within the encounter can be seen in figure 3.2. The data suggest that each participant shares these frames for the activity at hand. However, evidence also suggests that only some of the participants share the same schema for these frames.

Medical Interview Frame

Evidence regarding the medical interview frame is easily identifiable on the basis of the medical interview script, through the unfolding of this script via topic and question-answer sequences. Unlike the mock medical interview, in which only certain scenes were identifiable, the actual medical interview clearly contains aspects of all six scenes (repeated below for convenience) considered basic to a medical interview:

1. Opening
2. Medical history
3. Examination
4. Diagnosis
5. Consultation
6. Medical advice

While all six scenes are identifiable within the data, they do not necessarily occur in isolation from one another. Frequently, there is overlap between or among the various scenes. For example, the nurse, primarily, carries out the "opening" and "medical history" scene within the medical interview as she measures the baby's temperature and weight while seeking information about his shot records. Nevertheless, when the doctor enters, he is also interested in the medical history, as can be seen in lines 41 and 42 below:

Example 3.9*

41

M:

D: I walk in (?) big crowd!   **Is he sick?**

N:

C:

I:

I: LARGE MANY-PEOPLE C-R-O-W-D HERE   PRO.3 SICK PRO.3?

42

M: B-E-E-N SICK SO-SO UP-&-DOWN FOR ONE-WEEK NOW, FIRST STOMACH

D: Tell me what's wrong.   With what, =

N:

C:

I: Yeah he's been sick off and on . . .   for about a week now.
I: (waves for attention)

---

*In this example and most of the examples from the actual interview, the following abbreviations will be used: M = mother, D = doctor, N = nurse, C = child, I = interpreter.

In this example, the doctor initiates the topic (as well as a recent medical history) by asking, "Is he sick?" When the response is affirmative, the doctor elicits medical information with the utterance "Tell me what's wrong." Thus, the doctor initiates a medical history scene after one has been in progress with the nurse. Analysis of this type of scene overlap indicates that the medical history elicited by the nurse is a less recent and more generic kind of information, whereas the doctor elicits information about the recent history leading up to the current medical interview. In a similar way, throughout the medical encounter, each participant focuses on various aspects of the medical interview script, allowing the scenes to overlap and interweave throughout the course of the interview. The fact that these scenes share such an intricate and interdependent relationship could cause interactional problems. As in the case of the mock medical interview, the smooth running of the interview and the limited repair or renegotiation within the encounter indicate that all of the participants share a similar schema for medical interviews. Thus, linguistic evidence supports the existence of not only the medical interview frame, but also of the similarity of related schema.

Pediatric Examination Frame

Additional linguistic evidence, like the use of third-person pronominal reference and switches in linguistic register, indicates another layer to the medical interview: the pediatric examination frame. The use of indirect pronominal reference while speaking to one individual often indicates that a third party is being talked about. Schiffrin (1993) discusses situated meanings associated with the converse phenomenon, when one individual speaks *for* another. In her discussion, Schiffrin indicates that, depending on the circumstances, speaking for another can be viewed as either respectful or condescending to the party that has been spoken for. For example, Schiffrin points out the difference between when a secretary frees up her boss by making a phone call for him or her, and when "parents arrange play dates for their children who do not yet have the communicative competence to do so themselves" (235). Just as there are situations for which one individual speaks for another, there are situations during which individuals speak *about* one another. As Schiffrin's example illustrates, interacting with a child who does not have the communicative competence to respond is one such situation.

In the medical interview, the sick patient is a child. Undoubtedly, because of the patient's age, the doctor does not attempt to speak with him directly. Instead, the doctor speaks about the child in order to elicit the necessary information from his mother. The nurse also frequently refers to the child indirectly, as in the following example:

Example 3.10

2

Nurse: Let's put **him** on the scale

Clearly, the nurse is not speaking directly to the patient in this example. Such indirect references are made throughout the interview. The use of third-person pronominal reference indicates that the patient's ability to communicate directly is in question and thus represents at least one feature of a pediatric examination frame. However, there are numerous reasons that a patient might not be competent to communicate well during a medical interview. For instance, the patient might not be fluent in the language of the interview, or a drug or disease might influence the patient's ability to communicate. Hamilton (1994) discusses how an Alzheimer's patient's ability to communicate effectively can be hampered. For example, the patient might have an inability to distinguish information that is shared by an interlocutor from information that is new to the interlocutor. Hamilton makes the point that interactional responsibilities do not fall solely on the person whose communicative competence is in question. It is important to remember that supposedly "normal" communicatively competent individuals often contribute to interactional difficulties. Clearly, it is useful to examine additional linguistic features that signal that this medical interview can be framed as a pediatric examination. One such feature is linguistic register.

Linguistic register refers to language "varieties according to use" (Halliday, McIntosh, and Strevens 1964). According to Tannen and Wallat (1993), lexical, syntactic, and prosodic choices made with regard to addressees and the situation at hand are important indicators of frames. In their analysis of a pediatric examination, Tannen and Wallat (1982, 1983, 1987, 1993) identify various registers used by the pediatrician, including a conversational register with the mother and a teasing register or "motherese" used with the child. They describe the teasing register as distinguishable from the conversational register, indicating that it consists of "exaggerated shifts in pitch, marked prosody (long pauses followed by bursts of vocalization), and drawn out vowel sounds" (1993, 63). The teasing register is reported to occur during parts of the pediatric examination. For instance, during examination of the patient's ears, the doctor playfully implies that she is searching for different animals. The presence of a similar teasing register in the interpreted medical encounter serves as additional evidence of the pediatric examination frame.

The use of the teasing register can be seen throughout the interpreted medical interview. During examination of the patient's ears, the nurse (like the pediatrician in Tannen and Wallat's analysis) pretends to search for different creatures. This can be seen in example 3.11 below:

Example 3.11

86

N: Aw, sweetheart.
We're just looking to see—maybe Barney's in there,
y'know? (-?-). No, Barney's not in that ear today.

In this example the nurse playfully indicates that they are looking for Barney, a character in a children's television program, in the child's ear. Many of the vowels are elongated, and the nurse utters this with tremendous pitch variation. It is interesting to note that the teasing register is produced primarily by the nurse, and that the doctor never speaks to the baby at all. The pediatrician is juggling and balancing multiple frames, and it can be a burden on the physician to put the child "on hold" (Tannen and Wallat 1993, 68) while consulting with the parent and vice versa. In the interpreted medical encounter, the doctor and nurse might have accepted responsibility for managing different frames in an effort to reduce the doctor's burden. If that is the case, it might explain why the doctor does not speak to the child. It would be interesting to examine the same doctor and nurse with a variety of patients in order to determine if the observations made here are typical or not. It is conceivable that the doctor is experiencing extra burdens as a result of the interpreted encounter and research study frames addressed below.

Examination of linguistic features indicates an additional lamination of the medical interview frame. Participants' use of register shifts and of third-person pronominal reference with regard to the patient indicate that this medical interview has a layer that distinguishes it from other types of medical interviews. These linguistic features provide evidence of the pediatric examination frame. Due to the fact that there are no occurrences of major repairs or renegotiations, the participants appear to share similar schema regarding the pediatric examination frame.

Interpreted Encounter Frame

Analysis of the data indicates that all the participants frame this event as an interpreted encounter. Nevertheless, as in the case of the mock interview, there is some evidence that not all participants share the same schema regarding interpreted encounters. Unlike the mock medical interview, in the actual medical interview the Deaf participant and the interpreter appear to share similar schema regarding an interpreted encounter. Similar to the mock interview, this schema does not appear to match the schema of the medical care providers. Evidence of the unanimous existence of the interpreted encounter frame, as well as of the mismatches in schema, is shown in the following examples.

Primary linguistic evidence regarding the medical providers' interpreted encounter frame can be seen in the use of the third-person pronoun. Both the doctor and nurse frequently refer to the mother in the third person, and often add imperatives for the interpreter to direct comments to the mother. In the example 3.12, the nurse has just asked if the mother has brought the child's shot records:

Example 3.12

14

N: Just **tell her** we'd like to have them, because if she needs any forms or anything filled out, we need to have the dates.

In this example, the nurse clearly recognizes that she is not speaking directly to the Deaf woman. That is, by asking the interpreter to "tell her" the message, she has demonstrated an awareness that this is an interpreted encounter. The doctor makes similar reference in the example below:

Example 3.13

85

Doctor: **Ask her** to just hold his knees.

In this example, as in the previous one, the use of third-person reference serves as evidence that the speaker frames this as an interpreted encounter. Clearly, the doctor is aware that he is not communicating directly with the child's mother. The fact that both the doctor and the nurse make use of third-person pronouns when communicating with the mother not only indicates that they share the interpreted encounter frame, but also that they share a similar schema for that frame; that they are communicating with the Deaf mother indirectly. In contrast to this, neither the Deaf participant nor the interpreter seem to share this schema, despite the fact that there is evidence that both also frame this as an interpreted encounter.

Unlike the mock interview, the actual medical encounter contains no introduction or explanation regarding the interpreter and her presence. Nevertheless, the interpreter's utterances primarily consist of retellings of what interlocutors have recently said. Primarily, these retellings actually include the first-person pronoun, although the interpreter clearly does not mean to refer to herself, as in the following:

Example 3.14

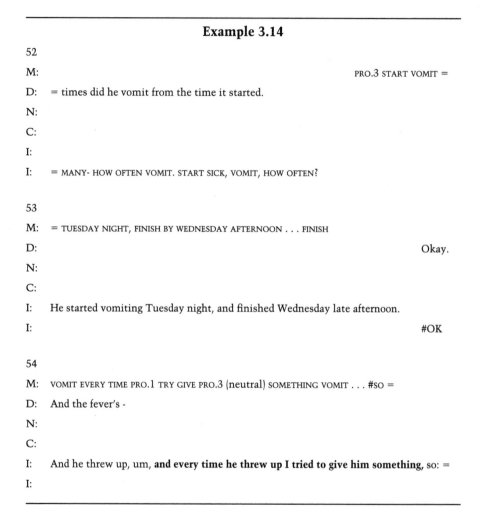

```
52
M:                                                         PRO.3 START VOMIT =
D:   = times did he vomit from the time it started.
N:
C:
I:
I:   = MANY- HOW OFTEN VOMIT. START SICK, VOMIT, HOW OFTEN?


53
M:   = TUESDAY NIGHT, FINISH BY WEDNESDAY AFTERNOON . . . FINISH
D:                                                               Okay.
N:
C:
I:   He started vomiting Tuesday night, and finished Wednesday late afternoon.
I:                                                               #OK


54
M:   VOMIT EVERY TIME PRO.1 TRY GIVE PRO.3 (neutral) SOMETHING VOMIT . . . #SO =
D:   And the fever's -
N:
C:
I:   And he threw up, um, **and every time he threw up I tried to give him something,** so: =
I:
```

The interpreter has never met the Deaf woman or her child prior to arrival at the doctor's office. Obviously, the interpreter does not mean that it was she herself who cared for the sick child on Tuesday and Wednesday. In this case, the first-person pronoun is used to refer to another participant, which indicates that the interpreter frames this event as an interpreted encounter. Further, the use of the first-person pronoun suggests a possible mismatch from the related schema evidenced by the doctor and nurse. The interpreter's schema for an interpreted encounter seems to be one of direct communication between the interlocutors, despite the fact that the interpreter is conveying the utterances for them. Hence, the interpreter's use of first-person reference is intended to apply to the original speaker (in this case, the signer) rather than to the interpreter herself.

A repair initiated by the doctor immediately following the previous example provides further evidence for the existence of this mismatch in schema between the medical practitioners and the interpreter:

Example 3.15

54

M: VOMIT EVERY TIME PRO.1 TRY GIVE PRO.3 (neutral) SOMETHING VOMIT . . . #SO =

D: And the fever's -

N:

C:

I: And he threw up, um, **and every time he threw up I tried to give him something,** so: =

I:

55

M: = PRO.1 GIVE-UP . . . E-V-E-N L-I-Q-U-I-D-S   PRO.1

D: **Yo 'points to interpreter) tried or she (points to mother) tried?**

N:

C:

I: = I don't know: I- (looks at doctor) I tried =

I: (waves)

56

M: PRO.1 + + (glances to interpreter) NO (taps doctor's arm) PRO.3 INTERPRETER-

D:

N:

C:

I: = to give him liquids too.

I: (taps mother's knee) PRO.1 TRY OR PRO.2 TRY?

57

M: = LET PRO.1 EXPLAIN. WHEN INTERPRETER TRUE INTERPRET, PRO.3 WILL =

D:

N:

C:

I: = Now let me explain. When the interpreter is interpreting, she will be speaking =

I:

58

M: = BE TALK A-S I-F PRO.3 NOT I-N ROOM PRO.3. TALK FOR PRO.1, #SO (?off screen)=

D: (chuckles)   Okay, gotcha.

N:

C:

I: = as if, she's not in the room.   She's speaking for me.   So, if it =

I:

59

M: = CONFUSE TRUE TALK PRO.1, A-S I-F PRO.3 PRO.1

D: I'm just interested in the pronoun, that's all.

N:

C:

I: = confuses you, the interpreter's really speaking as if-

I: PRO.1 (REALLY) INTEREST =

60

M: #OK PRO.1

D: You're not taking care =

N:

C: (cries)

I: = WORD "I" (i on chest) PRO.3 (left hand) I (i on chest)

61

M: NO PRO.1 RECENT MEET- (interpreter) #HER FIRST TIME =

D: = of him, you're just interpreting.

N:

C: (crying continues)

I: I just met =

I: NOT PRO.1, PRO.1 NOT TAKE-CARE -

62

M: = NOW.

D: okay   I've been in practice thirty-five years, I've =

N:

C: (screams then crying stops)

I: = her for the first time today, so

I: #OK   PRO.1 . . .   PRO.1 WORK++ =

The doctor initiates the repair in line 55, when he tries to clarify the interpreter's first-person pronominal reference. He supplements his own pronominal reference in this case with gestures, indicating exactly who is the referent of the second- and third-person pronouns.

The doctor's gestures indicate that he, in accordance with his apparent schema, is directing his comment to the interpreter (the referent of the second-person pronoun) and not to the Deaf woman. Similarly, the interpreter's utterances support her apparent schema of interpreted encounters as direct communication between the noninterpreter participants. Thus, she retells each interlocutor's utterances without any attempt to initiate an explanation of her own.

As in the case of the student interpreter, the professional interpreter's goal seems to be for the Deaf participant to respond, rather than to accept the status of ratified addressee. The Deaf woman's utterances indicate that, unlike the patient in the mock medical interview, she shares the interpreter's schema of what an interpreted encounter entails. That is, the Deaf woman not only understands the doctor's request for clarification, but she immediately responds to that request without any hesitation or expectation that the interpreter will also respond. She apparently trusts that the interpreter has continued to provide her with "direct" communication with the doctor. It is interesting to note the doctor's metalinguistic awareness in this example. In line 59, he himself indicates that his confusion is related to the issue of pronominal reference.

In the actual medical encounter, the fact that all participants share the interpreted encounter frame is similar to the findings regarding the mock medical interview. Moreover, the professional interpreter seems to share a similar schema with the student interpreter regarding this frame: that the interpreter is a service provider who prefers not to be involved in the doctor-patient "dyadic" interaction. Unlike the mock medical interview, in the actual medical interview, the doctor does not provide evidence of a schema in which the interpreter is a professional expert and colleague. Conversely, in lines 60–61 it becomes clear that the doctor's schema regarding the interpreter has been that she is a caretaker of the patient. Finally, although the Deaf patients in each interview frame the events as interpreted encounters, the Deaf patient in the mock interview demonstrates a distinct schema of the interpreter as advocate, whereas the Deaf patient in the actual medical interview shares a schema with the professional interpreter. Thus, although the fact that there are differing schema among the participants is true in both interviews, the nature of the mismatched schema is not the same.

Research Study Frame

The fact that the actual medical interview can be framed as a research study frame is evident through explicit reference to aspects of the event or to the researcher herself. The timing of these comments indicates that the participants not only share the frame for the event, but also that they share similar schema regarding the research study frame.

Of the participants in the actual medical encounter, the nurse provides the least amount of linguistic evidence of the research study frame and related schema. There are only two types of evidence that the nurse provides: comments regarding unusual aspects of the medical interview and limited interaction with the researcher or her camera. These two types of evidence provide only a limited indication of whether or not the nurse frames this event as a research study. As an example of the former, the nurse comments on the fact that the room really isn't big enough. The room is regularly used for medical interviews and is, thus, taken as big enough for a doctor, nurse, parent, child, as well as medical equipment such as a scale and sink. However, during data collection, this room houses an interpreter, a researcher, and a video camera as well. Thus, she comments in the example below:

Example 3.16

19

N: (enters) 'Scuse me. This room isn't really big enough, we looked
    for a larger room but we didn't have one available, so.

This comment addresses the fact that the room is overcrowded. It does not indicate the reason for that overcrowding, however. The nurse might make a similar comment with the additional presence of an interpreter or extended family members, even without the presence of a researcher. Thus, although this comment provides some evidence regarding conditions imposed by the research study (overcrowding), it is not sufficient to indicate that the nurse frames this event as a research study. Nevertheless, it is interesting to note that the nurse directs only one comment to the researcher, when her video equipment is in the way of the scale. The comment is made without the nurse making eye contact with, or glancing in the direction of, the researcher.

In example 3.17 the nurse is about to weigh the child. The video camera case is at the end of the table containing the scale, and the nurse reaches to move the camera case while commenting:

Example 3.17

2

  Nurse: I'm gonna move this for a second so he doesn't kick it for you.

The nurse does not look at the researcher, nor does she change her voice quality or prosody in any marked way. Nevertheless, since the camera case belongs with the camera being operated by the researcher, it seems likely that the referent of the second-person pronoun (and hence, the addressee) is the researcher. Aside from the contextual information regarding ownership of the camera case, there is no evidence that the nurse is addressing the researcher. In fact, it is entirely possible that the nurse does not recognize the case as a camera case, or does not know or believe that it is the researcher's. Given this possibility, there is no way to tell for certain who is the intended addressee of her utterance.

On the basis of the fact that the nurse interacts directly with all other participants, this example serves as additional evidence that the nurse frames this as a research study, and that her schema regarding such studies is that the presence of the researcher should be downplayed or ignored. Although the evidence demonstrated by the nurse is somewhat limited, evidence from other participants indicates that the doctor, the interpreter, and the mother frame the medical interview as a research study.

Like the nurse, the doctor comments on the crowded conditions of the examination room:

Example 3.18

41

  Doctor: I walk in (-?-) big crowd!

During the medical interview, the doctor does not direct utterances to the researcher. However, he does address the researcher at the end of the interview:

Example 3.19

226

    Doctor: You'll know it all. You keep comin' here, you'll become an expert.

Thus, the doctor indicates with this utterance that he is aware of the researcher's presence and that his schema allows him to talk with her. However, similar to the schema suggested by the nurse's lack of communication with the researcher, this utterance indicates that the doctor's schema regarding research studies is that the researcher should not be a part of the primary medical interview frame. The timing of the doctor's utterance suggests that it might be intended as a form of frame bracketing, occurring only after the medical interview frame has reached completion.

    The timing of utterances addressed to the researcher also serves as evidence of the frame and schema held by the interpreter and mother. It is important to note that the researcher is operating the video camera. As a result, she is not visible in the data collected. Nevertheless, her signed utterances are recognizable in part as a result of the mother's and the interpreter's eye gaze. When the researcher produces an utterance in ASL, the mother and interpreter can be seen to glance in the direction of the camera. The following example occurs during the initial part of the medical interview run by the nurse. Just prior to this example, the researcher has signed an utterance to the interpreter, asking her to move into view of the camera. However, the interpreter does not respond to this utterance until the nurse leaves the room:

Example 3.20

32

M:

N: Doctor should be in in just a few minutes (exits)

I: (to researcher) **Wha'd you say?**

I: DOCTOR COME FEW MINUTE

Throughout the interview, the interpreter interprets all the participants' utterances (English to ASL or ASL to English). It follows that if the researcher produces an utterance in either English or ASL, the interpreter would also interpret her utterance. The interpreter does not do that, however. Instead, the interpreter waits until the nurse leaves the room to respond directly to the researcher in English, "Wha'd you say?" This indicates that the interpreter does not view the researcher as she views the other participants. The researcher's utterance is treated as a part of another frame, the research study frame. The fact that the interpreter does not interpret the researcher's utterance, and that she does respond directly to the researcher during a frame break indicates that the interpreter has a schema associated with the research study frame that is similar to that of the doctor.

Like the interpreter, the child's mother also communicates directly with the researcher primarily during frame breaks. In the following example, the nurse has been conducting the preliminary examination. Just prior to the mother's utterance, the nurse has left the room to get a chart. During this period the child has been crying steadily. Approximately fifteen seconds after the nurse leaves the room, the mother (who is about five months pregnant with her second child) turns to the researcher and interpreter and addresses a comment to them:

Example 3.21

17

M:

D:

N: = So let me just (?) out there, I'll get it real quick.

C:

I:

I: (?) GO (?) NOTES GROW GROW-UP (?) FAST

18

                                (researcher laughs)   (researcher laughs)

M: [15-second pause] (to interpreter and researcher) PRO.1 HAVE SECOND ONE

     (laughs)   *And I'm having another one!*

D:

N: (leaves—gone for 28 seconds)

C:

I: **(laughs)**

I: (signs something but off camera)

19

                             (researcher laughs)

M: BOTH BOYS SAME **(laughs)**

     They're both boys, too!

D:

N: (enters) 'Scuse me. This room isn't really big enough, we looked for a larger room but =

C:

I: **(laughs)**

I: (? not visible) BIG ENOUGH (?) =

This comment receives laughter from both the researcher and the interpreter, and although both are off-camera at this point, it is clear from the mother's eye gaze that a brief conversation ensues among the three participants in the room. Although the nurse is gone for only twenty-eight seconds, there is time for the interpreter to comment (off-camera, in line 18) and for all participants to be laughing together as the nurse reenters the room. Once again, as the nurse returns, the interaction among the mother, interpreter, and researcher shifts. The mother generally does not gaze toward the researcher and only once directs a comment toward her during the time the medical interview frame is clearly active. This one comment can be seen in example 3.22. In this example, the mother waves briefly at the camera to entertain her son:

Example 3.22

110

M: (waves at camera) (looking at researcher) PRO.3 (baby) PISS-OFF =

D:

N:

C: (cries)

I: = THAT INDEX (neutral)

111

M: = SAME BECAUSE PRO.1 WAKE-UP PRO.3 U-P from POSS.3 (baby) N-A-P

D:

N:

C:

I: **He's really pissed off too because I woke him up from his nap.**

I:

After waving at the camera the mother gazes to the researcher and says that her son is upset because she interrupted his nap. The interpreter renders this comment in English (line 111). As the interpreter finishes her rendition, the mother gazes back and forth between the interpreter and the doctor. It looks as if the mother might have intended the comment to the researcher to be subordinated communication, ratifying the researcher as addressee but leaving the doctor unratified. It is not clear whether this is the case, although the mother does not address the researcher at all for the remainder of the encounter. This example raises a question regarding the issue of subordinated communication. Whether or not the mother has the opportunity to communicate in ASL with participants, or whether the doctor and nurse have an opportunity for subordinated communication in English is an issue that could be determined by the interpreter's choice of what to (or not to) render. Such a choice on the part of the interpreter has the potential of being more or less partial to one or another of various participants. How a variety of professional interpreters handle this issue is an area for future investigation. With regard to this study, the mother's limited interaction with the researcher, combined with rapid inclusion of interaction with the researcher during frame breaks, suggests that the mother frames the medical interview as a research study and that her schema of a research study entails the notion that one does not interact with the researcher as a part of the medical interview lamination of the event.

On the basis of the content of certain utterances that address the unusually crowded circumstances of this medical interview, as well as the limited number, and timing, of utterances directed toward the researcher, it is apparent that this medical encounter has been framed as a research study. Moreover, the evidence suggests that all the participants share similar schema regarding the research study frame. It is interesting to note that the interpreter and mother treat the researcher and interpreter in similar ways. Both are addressed and responded to primarily during breaks in the medical interview frame. For the mother and the interpreter, it appears that the research study frame and interpreted encounter frame share schematic elements in terms of the nonparticipation or noninvolvement of the researcher or interpreter in the task at hand.

A Mismatched Schema

Four layers of frames have been identified in the interpreted pediatric medical interview and discussed in terms of related schema. The medical interview and pediatric examination frames, the interpreted encounter frame, and the research study frame are characterized by a variety of linguistic features, including topic initiation, question-answer sequences, pronominal reference, linguistic register, and the content and timing of certain utterances.

Of the four frames examined, there is evidence that participants share similar schema regarding all but one: the interpreted encounter frame. Although not all participants frame the event as an interpreted encounter, the nurse and doctor demonstrate a schema in which they communicate with the interpreter about the Deaf participant, rather than one in which they communicate directly with the Deaf participant. This differs from the schema demonstrated by the Deaf participant and the interpreter. Both of these participants demonstrated a schema of direct communication among participants through the interpreter, rather than of communication with the interpreter herself.

The result of this apparent mismatch in schema is a problem area in the interaction. For example, the doctor requests clarification of the interpreter's use of the first-person pronoun. In his schema, the interpreter is seen as a caretaker of the child rather than as a professional service provider unknown to the Deaf participant and her family. His initiation of repair assists in clarifying that the referent of the interpreter's first-person pronoun is the mother.

The examination of the actual medical encounter with the professional interpreter has indicated that the frame and schema issues found in the mock medical encounter are not entirely unique for the student interpreter involved in a technical redoing. Thus, it would be worth exploring some of the similarities and differences in the interaction between frames and schema in the two cases under examination.

Comparison of Frames and Schema in the Two Cases of Interpreted Encounters

The dynamic interplay of frames and schema can allow people to understand (or misunderstand) interactive events. Examination of these two cases indicates that there are some similarities with regard to the interaction between frames and schema between the two cases. For example, the mismatches between participants' schema regarding interpreted encounters represents a similarity that is highly pertinent to the question of an interpreter's influence on interactive discourse.

In both the interpreted role play and the actual medical interview, a variety of linguistic features serve as evidence of frames and schema. These linguistic features include prosody, discourse sequences such as question-answer pairs, topic initiation, and repairs. In each case, linguistic features indicate that the participants share certain frames for the event. Although the frames for each case are not identical to the other, both cases include evidence of frames regarding the nature of the event, such as a role play or pediatric examination, and the interpreted encounter frame. In addition, both cases include evidence that all the participants share similar schema regarding all but the interpreted encounter frame. This could be due to the fact that medical interviews and even technical redoings are not uncommon types of interaction, whereas interpreted encounters are less familiar to the general population.

In both cases under examination, a hearing interlocutor requests information from the interpreter. In the role play the hearing interlocutor asks for information about the language, a question that could have been directed at the native signer in the group, but was not. Similarly, the doctor in the actual medical interview asks the interpreter for clarification of pronominal reference. This doctor also frequently refers to the Deaf interlocutor in the third person. In these examples, other participants talk about the Deaf participants (or their native language) rather than addressing them directly.

The communicative competence of people who are spoken for or about is an issue not just in interpreted encounters. For example, children and Alzheimer's patients are among those whose communicative competence comes into question in interaction. When hearing interlocutors speak about Deaf participants to an interpreter, do they question the Deaf participants' communicative competence? Does the hearing participant's schema categorize the Deaf participant with children or cognitively impaired patients? In what ways do the interpreter's utterances contribute to the participants perceptions of one another? These questions reflect some potential ramifications of the ways in which all participants (doctors, patients, and interpreters) align themselves to one another via their utterances. That is, the participation framework and the interpreter's place within it play important roles in the issue of interpreter neutrality and interpreter influence on an interaction.

4

Participation Frameworks

The Role of the Interpreter

IN ORDER to examine the sociolinguistic question of whether an interpreter can interpret interactive discourse without influencing it, this study has applied frame theory to two cases of interpreted encounters. Interpreters, like the other participants in the two cases under examination, bring their own individual frames and related schema to interpreted encounters. In each case, the mismatches in schema among participants were related to the interpreted encounter frame. The linguistic evidence of these mismatches, including pronominal reference, raises questions regarding the ways in which participants' utterances impact their relationship to, and perceptions of, one another. The relative participant structures that occur within an interpreted interaction can be examined in terms of Goffman's concept of *footing* (1981).

Participation Frameworks: Frames As Footing

Linguists have focused on essentially two aspects of frames. Some scholars, such as Fillmore (1976) and Tannen (1979), allude to frames in terms of activities, as in *commercial transactions* and the *film-viewing frame*. Frames have also been referred to in terms of participants, as in Fillmore (1976) and Chafe (1977). These two constructs are consistent with Goffman's discussion of the *framing* of events as multilayered and complex (1974); an event, such as a fight, can be *framed* as a transformed activity (i.e., play) and on the basis of participants (i.e., player vs. onlooker). It is the latter of the two, the participation framework, that provides a foundation for Goffman's notion of *footing.*

Goffman defines *footing* as "the alignment we take up to ourselves and the others present as expressed in the way we manage the production or reception of an utterance" (1981, 128). To clarify this definition, Goffman points out that traditional views of interaction, based on *speaker-hearer* dyads, are too simple to describe real interactive discourse. For example, although a ratified addressee might be identifiable, there might also be unratified addressees (bystanders) who access a conversation. Similarly, a *speaker* can be discussed in terms of more than one simple role.

Hearer roles include ratified and unratified status, and the question of whether or not someone is an addressed recipient. Speaker roles refer to the person who is the *principal, author,* and *animator* of utterances. Understanding these relationships within interactions can help clarify what linguistic evidence of *footing* might look like, and when shifts in footing occur. *Ratified* hearers are those who have an official place within a social encounter (Goffman 1981). Once ratified, an individual can choose whether or not to attend to the discourse. In addition, participants can choose to address certain individuals, leaving other ratified participants as *unaddressed* recipients. Thus, Goffman makes two relevant hearer distinctions: ratified-unratified addressee, based on access to official status within an encounter, and addressed-unaddressed recipient, which is reserved for ratified participants. The remaining possible hearer status, then, is the unratified participant who has access to the encounter. Goffman refers to such an individual as a *bystander.* Although Goffman discusses additional complexities for hearer status, by considering a variety of social situations, the divisions discussed here are sufficient for the purpose of this study.

Goffman describes three roles that a speaker can fulfill: *animator, author,* and *principal.* These three roles are not necessarily satisfied by the same person at the same time. A speaker generally functions as an *animator,* the "talking machine" (144) that actually produces an utterance. A speaker can also function as an *author* of an utterance, the originator of the content and form of the utterance.

While a speaker can function as both animator and author, it is possible for a speaker to function only as animator. For instance, when an actress speaks the lines of Shakespeare, she functions as the animator, but not the author of her utterances. Finally, Goffman describes the role of *principal* as the one who is responsible for or committed to what is being said. Thus, when someone reads a statement as a stand-in for a political figure, it is presumably the politician whose views are being expressed; the politician is, thus, the principal. By distinguishing among these three roles, what Goffman calls the *production format,* it can be seen that a speaker's relationship to utterances and addressees can be quite complex.

Understanding the production format within an encounter offers a way to analyze a speaker's alignment with other interlocutors. Each potential alignment represents a unique way of framing the encounter. For example, by quoting someone else's words, a speaker can imply a lack of responsibility for the content, denying *principal* status, even though the speaker is responsible for deciding the comment was worth reporting. Tannen (1986) provides a clear example of this. When one person tells another about a comment or criticism made by a third person, it is generally the third person who receives blame for the comment, rather than the one who has repeated it in the new context. Thus, it is the principal who is held accountable, rather than the animator. Evidence of various alignments is available through linguistic analysis. In fact, Goffman (1981) suggests that changes in footing are often evident through paralinguistic features of discourse. Researchers have applied the notion of footing to interactive discourse to identify a variety of linguistic features as evidence of footing and footing shifts.

Footing in Discourse

Gumperz (1982) discusses a variety of features that provide information regarding the footing between a speaker and addressees. In Gumperz' example of an African American graduate student who code-switches from Standard English to a black dialect, he points out that the student utters the sentence "Ahma git me a gig" with the singsong rhythm of a stereotyped African American character. Thus, the student is actually mocking his own role and making it clear to insiders that he is totally in control of his own situation (34). By borrowing the dialect and rhythmic prosody of a stock character, he is, in a way, not the principal of the utterance. This is an example of how code switching can represent a shift in footing.

Footing shifts have also been described as changes in participant frames. In examining a pediatric medical interview, Tannen and Wallat (1982, 1983, 1987, 1993) identify these footing shifts through changes in register. The pediatrician uses "motherese" with the child patient, a conversational register with the mother, and a reporting register to the video camera (which is recording the encounter for use by doctors-in-training). Goffman (1981) refers to this work as evidence of the complexities of footing shifts in interactive discourse.

In an examination of footing in news-interview discourse, Clayman (1992) found that interviewers maintained their own uninvolved neutrality by attributing strong opinions to others through the use of constructed dialogue of unnamed parties. Examples of this include indefinite or unspecific noun phrases, as in *"It* is said . . ."* (170) and *"critics on the conservative side* have said . . ." (171). Evidence that interviewers are striving to remain neutral is based on the occurrence of, and self-repairs toward, such constructions.

In an examination of footing within sermons, Smith discusses the use of a variety of forms, including pronouns, rhetorical question-answer sequences, and discourse markers (1993, 160). An example of the influence of pronoun reference occurs when preachers say "I think" or "It's interesting to me" versus "We can see." Smith suggests that the use of first-person singular identifies the preacher as author of the utterance, while use of first-person plural implies that the preacher speaks on behalf of the audience as well. The various strategies addressed by Smith appear to demonstrate ways in which preachers represent roles in the preaching task (for example, whether or not they present themselves as an authority or mediator).

The role of pronoun reference in footing shifts has also been found in the examination of footing in discourse of boys engaged in "sportscasting play." Hoyle (1993) describes shifts between first- and third-person pronouns as evidence that the boys are shifting footing. As they play Ping-Pong, the boys comment on the game as if it were a tennis match on television and, in so doing, refer to themselves in the third-person during "sportscaster talk" segments in the data: "They're hitting it back and forth!" (117). The occurrence of questions, response cries, asides, and explicit frame-bracketing with terms such as "Time out" all provide evidence of shifting footing between the boys animating their own utterances and animating utterances of an imaginary sportscaster.

The concept of speaking for another is explicitly addressed in Schiffrin (1993), in an analysis of sociolinguistic interviews. Schiffrin discusses shifts in footing as interactional moves. That is, in two examples in which one person speaks for another, one can be seen as helpful and supportive and an extension of help provided in daily activities. Another example can be seen as "putting words in someone's mouth," sharing information that might have been private, and seemingly doing so for some benefit of the speaker rather than the spoken for (238–39). Schiffrin demonstrates that just as linguistic markers might identify shifts in footing, footing shifts themselves can assist in the understanding of discourse.

Locker McKee (1992) examines footing in ASL lectures using Goffman's (1981) discussion of lectures as a base. Locker McKee addresses two types of footing in ASL lectures: quotations and asides. Locker McKee discusses many linguistic and paralinguistic cues that mark shifts in footing, including body leans and stepping to the side as spatial markers of changes in footing, and eye gaze to specify a particular addressee for asides. The use of performatives (for constructed dialogue), the lexical marker QUOTE, code switching, and prosodic changes are indicators of quotations, a shift in which the signer is animating an utterance attributed to another author. Locker McKee also discusses the use of STOP (this gloss referring to the one-or two-handed sign in which the signer's palm is forward facing the addressee) and INDEX-HOLD as discourse markers used to identify changes in footing.

Footing within English and ASL can be identified on the basis of prosodic, lexical, and other features. While these languages exhibit parallel features in this regard, the linguistic and paralinguistic markers within each language are different. These differences make ASL-English interpreted discourse a unique type of interaction in which to examine footing.

Footing in Interpreted Encounters

Goffman discusses the various roles that a speaker can fulfill in his description of production format. The production format involves unique dimensions when applied to the task of interpreting, a situation in which one individual relays the utterances of others. Few have attempted to analyze footing in interpreted interaction. However, Keith (1984), Edmondson (1986), and Wadensjö (1992) address the notion of production format in interpreted encounters, although they bring different perspectives to the task.

The notion of footing as applied to interpreting by Keith (1984) is very focused on the task of interpreting itself. Keith suggests that an interpreter operates within two distinct footings: translation of utterances and comprehension of utterances. The latter might result in requests for clarification or repetition, whereas the former refers specifically to rendering meaning equivalents. In this way, Keith seems to separate footings on the basis of authorship. That is, when translating, the utterance originates within someone else. When requesting clarification, the interpreter is the original author of the utterance.

Edmondson (1986) attempts to apply Goffman's conception of the three speakers' roles—animator, author, and principal—to the process of interpretation. In addition, he discusses Goffman's identification of hearer roles, addressee, hearer, and overhearer. Edmondson suggests that while interpreters are responsible for the formulation and production of utterances, they are not responsible for utterance meaning. Edmondson concludes that interpreters are not involved in interactions, and that they are neither speakers nor hearers; rather, they depend on a completely unique cognitive process that requires both speaking and hearing be accomplished simultaneously.

Wadensjö draws a different conclusion. In her data-based research, Wadensjö discusses the interpreted encounters as "conditioned by the *co-presence* of at least . . . three persons, and one of these (the Dialogue Interpreter) characteristically relays between the others" (1992, 65). The interpreter's talk is analyzed as two types, relaying and coordinating talk. Through an examination of the relaying done by interpreters, Wadensjö finds that interpreters' renditions sometimes closely parallel an original participant's utterance, sometimes contain somewhat more or less information than the original, sometimes summarize prior talk, and sometimes the interpreter's utterance is not based on a prior utterance. Based on the various types of renditions, Wadensjö concludes that interpreters do not function simply as "translation machines" (72).

In examining an interpreter's coordinating function, Wadensjö again identifies a taxonomy. For example, an interpreter might ask for clarification, prompt a response or turn from a primary party, explain what one party or another means, or explain that one party does not appear to understand another. In addition, Wadensjö points out that an interpreter influences the coordination of talk simply by relaying utterances; the course of a conversation is influenced, in part, by the content and form of the interpretation.

Footing, as it has been applied to interpreted interaction, can be seen to reflect two different views of the interpreter. Edmondson's work, which is not data-based, seems to reflect the more traditional notion of interpreter as an uninvolved relayer of messages. Keith and Wadensjö seem to view interpreters in a more interactive light, shifting footings as they attempt to comprehend and relay conversation. The ways in which interpreters negotiate footing shifts is still a relatively unexplored area.

Footing within Interpreter-Generated Utterances

Research regarding footing in English and ASL discourse provides some examples of the types of linguistic evidence of footing that can be found in conversational interaction. Research regarding the potential footings in interpreted encounters has focused, in part, on the various potential footings within an interpreter's talk. For example, Wadensjö (1992) describes an interpreter's interpretation as one of two types of utterances that are generated by interpreters. She describes interpretations as *renditions*, indicating that while a rendition has originated outside of the interpreter, the interpreter still authors the form and content of that rendition (in the choice of form, for instance). Just as an interpreter provides renditions of what participants say, an interpreter can also omit another participant's talk. Wadensjö refers to this as a *lack of rendition*. A lack of rendition is distinguishable from the second type of utterance identified by Wadensjö, which is *nonrenditions*. Where a lack of rendition refers to an omission, a nonrendition is an additional utterance, generated by the interpreter, that has not originated with anyone else.

Although some researchers have begun to explore the negotiation of footing in interpreted encounters, no one has examined footing in ASL-English interpreted interaction. Moreover, in signed-spoken language interpreting there is often an added complexity of potential bimodal utterances on the part of the interpreter.[1] The purpose of this portion of the study is to analyze the two ASL-English interpreted encounters in order to identify and categorize evidence of footing. In order to examine ways in which interpreters influence an interaction, the primary focus of this analysis will be on interpreter-generated utterances, paying particular attention to the form and function of the interpreters' utterances that are nonrenditions of spoken or signed language.

Footing in Interpreted Interaction: Mock Medical Encounter
Examination of interpreter-generated nonrenditions in the mock medical interview reveals that interpreters do contribute to interactional discourse. In these data, the interpreter frequently treats the Deaf interlocutor as a ratified addressee, excluding the hearing interlocutor. Conversely, there is only one utterance for which the interpreter treats the doctor as a ratified addressee while excluding the Deaf interlocutor. Most utterances directed to the hearing interlocutor are both spoken and signed, allowing the Deaf interlocutor to access the utterance as an unaddressed recipient. Thus, the interpreter establishes different footings between herself and each of the other participants.

The total number of utterances produced by the student interpreter is 117. Of these utterances, 102 are clearly motivated by the utterances of other participants and are classifiable as renditions. Thus, the total number of interpreter-generated nonrenditions is 15, representing 13 percent of her utterances. The analysis of this percentage of the interpreter's discourse, and its influence within the interaction, is the focus here. Of the 15 nonrenditions, 11 are directed to the Deaf patient and are signed only, thus denying the hearing interlocutor access as a ratified unaddressed recipient (see table 4.1). One utterance is directed to the doctor only and is spoken but not signed. Interestingly, this utterance is actually a repetition of an utterance generated by the Deaf interlocutor. Because the Deaf patient signs the comment only once, but the interpreter decides to repeat it, the repetition is considered here to be an interpreter-generated utterance. For 3 of the 15 interpreter-generated utterances, the interpreter attempted to sign and speak simultaneously. For each of these utterances, the ratified addressed recipient was the hearing interlocutor, and the combination of speaking and signing created a footing in which the Deaf interlocutor was a ratified but unaddressed recipient.

These results indicate that the interpreter creates different footings with each interlocutor. She almost never allows the Deaf interlocutor to become an unratified addressee. However, the hearing interlocutor frequently receives unratified status on the basis of the interpreter's footings. In order to get a better sense of the footings the interpreter creates, and how they are situated within the interaction, it is useful to categorize the interpreter's footing types and their functions.

Table 4.1 Occurrences of Interpreter-Generated Nonrenditions in Mock Medical Interview

	N	Signed and Spoken (%)	Spoken Only (%)	Signed Only (%)
Number of Occurrences	15	3 (20.0%)	1 (6.7%)	11 (73.3%)

One of the ways in which Goffman distinguishes footing is on the basis of speaker roles. As described earlier, a speaker might employ any or all of the three roles of animator, author, and principal. The interpreter's utterances, for which the interpreter is primary author, seem to vary in terms of the principal role. Certain interpreter-generated utterances seem to function as a part of the interpretation process. That is, some information is available within the interaction and originates among the interlocutors, but for some reason the interpreter must generate an utterance in order to fulfill the goal of relaying that information. For at least some relayings the interpreter functions as animator and author, but not as principal. For other interpreter-generated utterances, the interpreter appears to be managing some aspect of the interaction. For these utterances the interpreter appears to fulfill all three speaker roles.

Relayings

When an interpreter relays what other people say, generally the original speaker can be thought of as a primary author while the interpreter is a secondary author and animator. Thus, relayings for which the interpreter is primary author are somewhat unique. Examination of the mock medical interview reveals three types of relayings where the interpreter is clearly the primary author. These types include source attribution, explanations, and repetitions (see table 4.2).

Source Attribution

In interactional discourse, people are generally able to identify speakers on the basis of voice recognition and location. When dis-

Table 4.2 Occurrences of Relayings in Mock Medical Interview

	N	Source Attribution (%)	Explanations (%)	Repetitions (%)
Number of Occurrences	9	4 (44.4%)	4 (44.4%)	1 (11.1%)

course is funneled through a single individual, the interpreter, information regarding the location and identity of the source (the original animator) is not inherently discourse-bound. In other words, the interpreter can relay the content of the discourse without necessarily imparting the source of that content. Moreover, if the interpreter engages in self-generated utterances, there is potential confusion over whether a particular utterance has originated from the interpreter or another source. Thus, it is not surprising to find that some of the interpreter-generated utterances are devoted to source attribution. Of the fifteen utterances, four specifically identify the original animator of the upcoming utterance (see table 4.2). The interpreter appears to fulfill all three speaker roles for this utterance, since only the interpreter has contributed this information to the discourse. If the interpreter provides incorrect information about the source, it is the interpreter who is responsible for the incorrect content. Thus, the interpreter is not only animator and primary author, but also principal for such utterances.

The most frequent form of source attribution is a single indexical point in the direction of the speaker. In example 4.1 below, the interpreter has just finished introducing herself to the doctor and patient, and the doctor begins the medical interview:

Example 4.1

3

P:

D: And how are you feeling this morning?

I:

I: (point right)   HOW FEEL ALL RIGHT MORNING?
      She said,   *"How are you feeling? Are you all right this morning?"*

The point to the right is directed toward the doctor. Just prior to this example the interpreter has been functioning as author and principal of her own introduction, and the pointing indicates a shift in footing

such that the doctor is the primary author and principal of the upcoming utterance. Index pointing in ASL is comparable to the use of
pronouns as markers of footing in English (cf. Hoyle 1993; Smith
1993).

It is interesting to note that all four occurrences of source attribution are directed to the Deaf interlocutor. The interpreter never
authors any utterance designed to clarify for the hearing interlocutor whether an utterance originated from the patient or the interpreter. In addition, although the interpreter provides this type of information to the patient, she does not do so consistently. That is, for
every utterance produced by the interpreter, an inherent question regarding the source of that utterance exists (is it motivated by the interpreter or by another participant?). Thus, it is noteworthy that of
117 utterances for which source could be attributed, the interpreter
attributes the source only 4 times. Future research might seek to
identify whether professionally certified interpreters provide source
attribution, whether they do so consistently, and if not, what circumstances elicit such utterances.

Explanations
Explanations are a second type of relaying provided by the student
interpreter. There are two types of explanations in the data: those in
which the interpreter explains event-related information, and those
in which the interpreter explains why the doctor has spoken to the
interpreter as a ratified addressee. An example of the former can be
seen in example 4.2, in which the interpreter informs the patient
that a third person, a nurse, has just entered the room:

Example 4.2

25

P:

D: Uh, I do have a list of uh, food that I'd like you to . . . try to stick to-

N: Excuse me, doctor, can I see =

I:

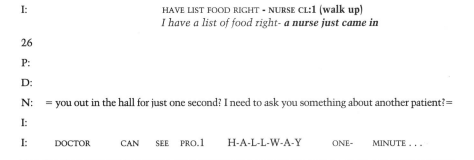

After the interpreter explains that the nurse has entered, she goes on to relay what the nurse has said to the doctor. This type of explanation occurs once in the data.

The second type of explanation occurs when the doctor directs an utterance to the interpreter as addressee. An example of this occurs when the doctor asks the interpreter how to sign a word:

Example 4.3

22

D: What is- is there a sign for ulcer?

I: PRO.3 PRO.1 SIGN FOR U-L-C-E-R PRO.2? ASK-PRO.1 QUESTION
     She asked me, "What's your sign for ulcer?" She asked me a question.

The interpreter signs the question, including the footing shift on the part of the doctor in which she shifts from treating the interpreter as an unratified addressee or bystander to a ratified addressee. The interpreter explains to the patient that the doctor has asked her a question.

Another example of this type of explanation occurs in example 4.4. In this example, the doctor is responding to a question from the patient. When the interpreter accidentally touches the doctor's arm while signing "WELL," the doctor stops in the middle of her explanation, pauses, and asks the interpreter if there is a problem (line 57):

Example 4.4

54

P: = AWKWARD ME

D: Well-   y'know it just depends on whether you really =

I: = on coffee. If I don't have it, I'm a- I'm a wreck.

I: UH =

55

P:

D: = wanna heal or not, uh, r- as I said before, right now this isn't a big problem an ulcer is =

I:

I: = TRUE DEPEND PRO.1 WANT HEALTH . . .   TRUE   U-L-C-E-R =

56

P:

D: = just a little open sore. If you don't wanna follow these lists, or take the medicines, then =

I:

I: = NOTHING.   SUPPOSE NOT FOLLOW LIST, =

57

P:

D: = there- . . . **is there a problem?** Oh. -then it can become infected and then you do have a problem.

I: **'scuse me.**

I: = WELL . . .   **EXCUSE. PRO.1 TOUCH (to doctor) Doctor-LOOK-AT-interpreter** . . . THEN CAN
     WORSE.=
               Excuse me. I touched the doctor and she was, like, looking at me.

The interpreter apologizes to the doctor and then explains to the patient what just happened. Although the apology is both spoken and signed, the explanation is rendered only in ASL. The doctor, unaware of this subordinated communication, has continued with the medical interview. Part of the doctor's utterance is not rendered in the interpretation as a result of the overlap. The data contain two occurrences of this type of explanation.

The two types of explanations in these data include explanations about the event and explanations regarding why the hearing interlocutor has spoken to the interpreter. Given a larger body of data, it would be interesting to examine whether or not explanations are ever provided to hearing interlocutors, and if so, under what circumstances.

Repetition

The last type of relaying to be discussed consists of repetitions. Obviously, some repetitions in the data originate from participants other than the interpreter. However, there is one example in the data in which the interpreter, as secondary animator, decides to reanimate the utterance apparently due to an overlap in the talk:

Example 4.5

40

P:

D: = have milk, but have it with a meal, and try to limit how much milk you have, so that you're =

I:

I: CAN HAVE . . .   WITH FOOD . . .   =

              You can have milk with food   *but try to limit*

41

P: LIMIT? MEAN LIMIT? NOT UNDERSTAND LIMIT.
              Limit? What do you mean by that? I don't understand what you mean.

D: = not just . . . uh, y'know, maybe drinking a gallon of milk on an empty stomach.

I: **What do you mean, limit? What do you mean limit?**

I: = TRY LIMIT + +

The repetition occurs in the interpreter's English discourse in line 41. It is interesting to note that the Deaf interlocutor responds at an appropriate moment in the interpreter's discourse, after she signs "LIMIT" (line 41). His response consists of a request for clarification of the doctor's indication that he should limit his milk intake. His request is translated by the interpreter into a single English question, "What do you mean, limit?" However, the interpreter necessarily lags behind the doctor's speech; in line 41 the interpreter is still animating what the doctor said in line 40. When the Deaf interlocutor, who, from his perspective, does not interrupt the conversation, is immediately reanimated by the interpreter, the rendition occurs during the doctor's utterance, causing an overlap in the English dialogue. The doctor does not yield her turn. When the doctor does complete her turn, the interpreter then reanimates her interpretation of the patient's question a second time (though he does not pause and then repeat his utterance) apparently so that it can be heard by the doctor. In this manner, the interpreter has taken responsibility for resolving the overlap, by removing it. If she did not, it is conceivable that another of the interlocutors would have taken responsibility for the repetition. For example, the doctor might have asked the patient what he just said, a question that the interpreter could have interpreted. Conversely, if the doctor did not respond to his question, the patient could have authored a repetition himself. Roy (1989a) discusses the role of the interpreter in turn-taking. An examination of the affects of footing shifts on turn-taking in interpreted interaction would be another area for future research.

The most common of the interpreter footings that occur as relaying tasks are source attribution and explanations. In considering the Interpreter's Paradox, it is interesting to note that at least one of these categories, source attribution, appears to be a required component of interpreted interaction. That is, interlocutors cannot make sense of an interaction if they do not know who is responsible for the utterances. Clearly, some interpreter-generated nonrenditions are essential to the task of interpreting interactive discourse.

Interactional Management

In addition to relaying information about what is said or what is happening within an event, an interpreter's nonrenditions can also

Table 4.3 Occurrences of Interactional Management in Mock Medical
Interview

	N	Introductions (%)	Responses to Questions (%)	Interference (%)
Number of Occurrences	6	2 (33.3%)	3 (50.0%)	1 (16.7%)

be related to the structure of the interpreted encounter. The footing types that occur within this category can be classified as introductions, responses to questions, and interference (see table 4.3).

Introductions

A professional interpreter will become accustomed to interacting with professionals from various fields, including medical practitioners with a variety of specialties. It is less common, however, for these other professionals to have experience working with interpreters. As a result, participants in a given interaction might not understand who the interpreter is or what particular task he/she will fulfill without some sort of introduction.

In the mock interview, the interpreter introduces herself by signing and speaking simultaneously (example 3.5). This yields a footing in which the interpreter is addressing both interlocutors. The code choice is somewhat awkward, and evidence of this appears in the form of errors or self-repairs in both languages, as can be seen in example 4.6 below:

Example 4.6

1

P:

D: Oh, you're the interpreter for today.

I: . . . and I'm gonna be the sign lang- language interpreter for today.

I: POSS. I SIGN LANGUAGE INTERPRETER LANGUAGE NOW. PRO.1, PRO.3, PRO.1 OH INTERPRETER =
      I'll be the sign language interpreter- language for today. I- She said, "Oh, I'll be the =

2

P: (nods)

D: It's nice to meet you.

I: Thank you, it's nice to meet you too.

I: NOW PRO.1, #OH #OK. PRO.1 - NICE MEET PRO.1. THANKS NICE MEET -TO (doctor) SAME.
      interpreter for today, oh, okay." It's nice to meet me. Thanks, it's nice to meet you, too.

In line 1 the interpreter treats both interlocutors as ratified addressees. In line 2, the interpreter responds to the doctor as they exchange greetings, resulting in an unaddressed recipient status for the patient. It is interesting to note that this footing is apparently noticed by the Deaf interlocutor, and in a later reenactment of the interview,[2] the introductions are initiated by the patient, not by the interpreter (see example 4.7):

Example 4.7

D:

P: HELLO PRO.1 INTRODUCE PRO.3 POSS.1 INTERPRETER (name) PRO.3 (nods)
      Hello. I'd like to introduce you to the interpreter. Her name is -.

I: Hi. I'd like to introduce you to the interpreter. Her name is -.

I:

In example 4.7 the Deaf patient handles the introduction of the interpreter. Thus, the interpreter does not generate any nonrenditions, and does not have to make code choices that start the interview on any particular footing. Introductions can be handled in other ways as well. For instance, the interpreter could choose to introduce herself in one language at a time. Each of these options seems to result in a different footing, whether interpreter-initiated or not. Future research regarding the impact of the various footings on different genres of interaction could clarify the impact various types of footing have with regard to the Interpreter's Paradox.

Responses to Questions

Another type of structural footing shift occurs when questions are directed to the interpreter. These questions can come from either the hearing or the Deaf interlocutor, and examples of both occur in the data, though they are somewhat different in character.

In the mock medical interview, the doctor directs questions to the interpreter during the course of the interview. This was seen in example 3.7 and is repeated here as example 4.8 for convenience:

Example 4.8

22

P:

D: What is- is there a sign for ulcer?

I:

I: PRO.3   PRO.1   SIGN =
                                      She asked me, "What's your sign

23

P: (hand flip)
                              (Whatever.)

D: No, huh?. . . Oh, okay =

I: Umm . . .

I: FOR U-L-C-E-R PRO.2? . . . ASK-TO (interpreter) QUESTION. NO SIGN? ASK-TO (interpreter)
     for ulcer."   *She asked me a question.*   *There isn't one? She asked me.*

In this example, the interpreter does not respond to the doctor's question. She interprets what the doctor said, and adds her explanation, but all this is done in ASL and is not accessible to the doctor. Thus, the interpreter shifts footing, but not in harmony with the doctor's shift to interpreter as an addressed recipient. This example differs somewhat from those occurrences in which the patient asks a question of the interpreter.

There are two differences between the previous example and example 4.9 below. First, the patient never asks a question of the interpreter during the course of the interview. The only time the patient treats the interpreter as an addressed recipient is when the doctor is temporarily called out of the room. The second difference between these two examples is that the interpreter responds to the patient with a much different footing. While the interpreter does not comply with the patient's request, she does provide an answer to his question, filling the empty slot in the patient-initiated adjacency pair (Schegloff and Sacks 1973):

Example 4.9

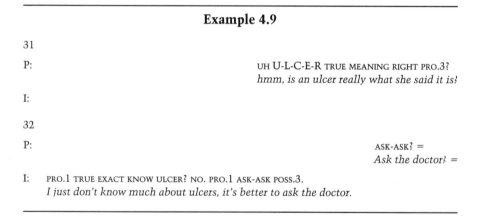

31

P: UH U-L-C-E-R TRUE MEANING RIGHT PRO.3?
                                          hmm, is an ulcer really what she said it is?

I:

32

P: ASK-ASK? =
                                                     Ask the doctor? =

I: PRO.1 TRUE EXACT KNOW ULCER? NO. PRO.1 ASK-ASK POSS.3.
     I just don't know much about ulcers, it's better to ask the doctor.

In example 4.9, the interpreter accepts the footing established by the patient and responds to his question. In these data, there are three occurrences in which the patient asks the interpreter a question and she generates a response, albeit without complying with the request for information or assistance. In addition, there is one example in which the doctor asks the interpreter a question. In this example, the interpreter never responds to the doctor, but tries to elicit a response from the patient by explaining the situation. This footing type is included in the taxonomy on the basis of function (explaining) as are the other types of footing that occur in the data (see table 4.3).

Interference
The last type of footing shift identifiable in the mock medical interview occurs as a result of the physical environment. During the course of the interview, the interpreter accidentally touches the doctor's arm while signing. This segment of the transcript is repeated as example 4.10 below:

Example 4.10

57

P:

D: = there- . . . is there a problem? oh. -then it can become infected and then you do have a problem.

I: 'Scuse me.

I: = WELL . . .   EXCUSE. PRO.1 TOUCH (to doctor) doctor-LOOK-AT-interpreter . . . THEN CAN
     WORSE. =
                    Excuse me. I touched the doctor and she was, like, looking at me.

This segment of the data, seen in example 4.4, includes an explanation within the utterance. However, prior to the explanation the interpreter shifts footing by code switching and simultaneously signing and speaking a comment directed to the doctor as an addressed recipient, with the patient as unaddressed recipient. The interpreter shifts footing by excusing herself for accidentally touching the doctor. It is interesting to note that after excusing herself, the interpreter does not provide an explanation to the doctor for why the doctor was seemingly tapped on the arm.

The types of interference currently under discussion reveal footing shifts resulting from changes in the physical environment (i.e., being seated next to someone while signing). These types of interference are similar to Hoyle's discussion of footing shifts resulting from interference (1993, 128), as when a dog gets in the way of a Ping-Pong game and interrupts children engaged in sportscaster talk.

Relayings and Interactional Management in the
Mock Medical Interview

The two different categories of footing shifts, relayings and interactional management, are determined on the basis of fifteen interpreter-generated nonrenditions within the data. Of the fifteen utterances, six functions have been identified, three categorized as relayings, and three as related to management of the interaction. The existence of these utterances and the variety of footings that they represent suggest that the student interpreter is one of the interactional participants. However, the function of many of the footings appears to be related to the interpreter's goal of providing access to the interaction while minimizing participation in it. Nevertheless, it is interesting to note that almost three-quarters of the interpreter's nonrenditions are directed to the Deaf participant only, and are not accessible to the hearing participant. Having examined the student interpreter's nonrenditions, the next question is whether or not the professional interpreter exhibits nonrenditions, and if she does, what types of footings they represent.

Footing in Interpreted Interaction: Actual Medical Encounter

Like the student interpreter in the mock medical encounter, the professional interpreter in the actual medical encounter contributes nonrenditions to the interactional discourse. As in the mock interview, the interpreter frequently treats the Deaf interlocutor as a ratified addressee while excluding the hearing interlocutors as a result of code choices. However, unlike the student interpreter, the professional interpreter never attempted to both speak and sign simultaneously while in the presence of either the doctor or the nurse. Thus, the professional interpreter's nonrenditions, on the basis of language code, treat either the Deaf mother or the hearing medical practitioner (but never both at the same time) as ratified addressees. Although the nature of the footings differ, the professional interpreter, like the student interpreter, establishes different footings between herself and each of the other participants.

The professional interpreter produces a total of 387 utterances. Of these utterances, 358 are renditions of discourse produced by other participants. Thus, there are a total of 29 interpreter-generated nonrenditions in the actual medical interview. The interpreter's nonrenditions represent 80 percent of her utterances. The focus here will be on the analysis of this percentage of the interpreter's discourse and its influence on participant alignments within the interaction. As in the case of the mock medical interview, a majority of these utterances are directed to the Deaf interlocutor and are signed only (see table 4.4). Four of the utterances are spoken only. Of the 4, 1 is directed to the doctor, one to the nurse, and 2 are directed to the researcher during a period when neither the doctor or nurse is present. These last 2 utterances occur during a frame break, since the linguistic evidence suggests that the participants view this period as an out-of-frame (that is, the interpreted encounter frame) activity. Finally, 3 of the 29 utterances are both spoken and signed. These occur during the interpreted encounter frame-break, while the interpreter is communicating with the Deaf mother and the hearing researcher. Unlike the "simultaneously" produced utterances generated by the student interpreter, in which the hearing and Deaf participants were all ratified but only the hearing participant was an addressed recipient, in the three occurrences generated by the professional interpreter both participants appear to be both ratified and addressed. Since some of the interpreter's utterances are both spoken and signed, while others are one or the other, this represents interesting code switches on the part of a native bilingual. Although it is beyond the scope of this study, it would be interesting

Table 4.4   Occurrences of Interpreter-Generated Nonrenditions in Actual Medical Interview

	N	Signed and Spoken (%)	Spoken Only (%)	Signed Only (%)
Number of Occurrences	29	3 (10.3%)	4 (13.8%)	22 (75.9%)

to determine what code choices native bilinguals who are hearing make when communicating with Deaf and hearing bilinguals, and what the function of such footing shifts might be in noninterpreted discourse.

These findings are similar to the results of the mock medical interview analysis. For example, the interpreter-generated nonrenditions consist primarily of utterances directed to the Deaf participant and are inaccessible to the doctor or nurse. However, since a footing is a highly situated part of an interaction, it is critical to examine the form and function of the nonrenditions generated by the professional interpreter. As in the case of the student interpreter, the professional interpreter's utterances under examination fulfill two goals: relaying and interactional management. However, the specific functions within each of these two categories are not identical to the first case.

Relayings

Most of the relayings produced by an interpreter consist of renditions. However, an examination of the interpreters' nonrenditions reveals that some clearly serve a relaying function. In the actual medical interview, the utterances categorized as relayings consist of two of the functions found in the mock medical encounter: source attribution and repetitions. In addition, the professional interpreter's nonrenditions include requests for clarification (see table 4.5).

Table 4.5   Occurrences of Relayings in Actual Medical Interview

	N	Source Attribution (%)	Repetitions (%)	Requests for Clarification (%)
Number of Occurrences	10	3 (30.0%)	4 (40.0%)	3 (30.0%)

Source Attribution

Monolingual native English interlocutors are able to identify speakers on the basis of voice recognition and location; therefore, discourse funneled through a single source (the interpreter) does not inherently include such information. However, since that single source also generates nonrenditions, there is the potential for confusion over who is the original author of each utterance produced by the interpreter. Therefore, it is not surprising to find that source attribution is one type of utterance found in both the interpreted mock and actual medical interviews. What is surprising, perhaps, is the relatively limited number of occurrences of source attribution in the actual medical interview. Only three of the interpreter's nonrenditions attribute source. The attribution of source takes two forms: pointing and body shifting.

In the following example, the interpreter incorporates a body shift as well as a point in the direction of the doctor, who is the original author of the utterance. At this point in the interaction, the doctor and nurse are examining the child, who is crying:

Example 4.11

94

M:

D: Well, let's have-

N: **Oh, darn it.**

C: (crying)   (coughs)

I:

I: #WELL

95

M:

D: He's cutting four teeth and that's contributing to the mucus, =

N:

C: (cries)

I:

I: #OH D-A-R-N #IT   (shifts to side) #HE HAVE FOUR EYETEETH C-U-T =

96

M:

D: = and it's easy for mucus to get in, behind the eardrums and and, so teething infants frequently =

N:

C:

I:

I: = INDEX (doctor) THAT PROVIDE SOME M-U-C-O-U-S THAT EASY M-U-C-O-U-S BEHIND =

97

M:

D: = have that.

N:

C:

I:

I: = E-A-R-D-R-U-M-S #SO TEETH BABY THAT TEETH OFTEN HAVE THAT

In the first line, the interpreter begins by fingerspelling an utterance originally authored by the nurse, "Oh, darn it," and then goes on to provide a rendition of the doctor's utterance regarding the child's eyeteeth. Just prior to beginning the rendition of the doctor's utterance, the interpreter shifts her body slightly to the right. In this manner, she is able to differentiate between the two English speakers. However, the body shift alone does not distinguish which of the two is speaking, merely that the original author has changed, thus, the interpreter includes a point in the direction of the doctor in the second line. The interpreter is able to make a distinction between the two speakers, including two discourse-relevant pieces of information not otherwise accessible to the Deaf interlocutor: that the primary author has shifted, and identification of the primary author.

The use of the body shift is comparable to what Wadensjö refers to as reported speech in interpreter's renditions. When the words or

actions of more than one individual are being reported or constructed, body shifting is a strategy used for distinguishing multiple
characters in ASL narratives.[3] In addition, both Winston (1991) and
Locker McKee (1992) discuss the use of body shifts in ASL lectures
as markers of changes in footing. It is interesting to note the use of a
narrative discourse strategy on the part of the interpreter. Since the
interpreter is a single individual relaying into one language all the
utterances originating in another, she is functioning somewhat like
a narrator who is constructing the dialogue of a specific event. The
difference between the interpreter's narrative and "conventional"
narrative discourse is that the interpreter is narrating an event while
it occurs in the present time and space (cf. Wolfson 1979).

In the previous example, the interpreter used a combination of
linguistic devices to attribute the source of the utterance being rendered. However, some examples include no attribution of source. In
the following example, the doctor, nurse, and mother all are involved in the examination of the child. The child is crying loudly:

Example 4.12

86

M:

D: Ask her to just hold his knees.

N: Aw, sweetheart.

C: (crying)   (wails)

I:

I: JUST HOLD K-N-E-E-S   SWEETHEART

The interpreter provides a rendition of the doctor's utterance, followed by a rendition of the nurse's utterance. No marker is used to
indicate to the Deaf participant that the same person did not originally author both utterances. Although the doctor and nurse are not
in the room at the same time throughout the duration of the interview, there is always potential confusion as to who is the originator
of a given utterance. Not only is the hearing researcher present as a

potential English speaker, but also the interpreter mixes renditions with nonrenditions during the interview. Thus, every utterance produced by the interpreter can be questioned regarding source. For this reason, the omission of source indication is an interesting finding in the actual interview. Is source information not pertinent to Deaf consumers? Is the determination of source available through other means, such as looking to see whose mouth is moving? The presence or absence of source attribution, and its potential impact on interactive discourse, is an area for further investigation with a larger body of data.

In keeping with the identification of a limited amount of source attribution in ASL for the Deaf interlocutor, a limited amount of source attribution is provided in English for the hearing interlocutors. Just as the potential exists for the Deaf participant to be confused between nonrenditions and renditions, or to whom original authorship of a given rendition is attributable, hearing participants can also become confused about who is the author and/or principal of an utterance. In example 3.15 (repeated here as example 4.13), the doctor becomes confused about who the principal was for a given utterance:

Example 4.13

55

D: You (points to interpreter) tried or she (points to mother) tried?

In this example, the doctor specifically asks for clarification regarding the source: "You tried or she tried?" The doctor appears to be uncertain as to whether the interpreter is providing a rendition of the mother's utterance or a nonrendition for which the interpreter herself is the sole author. Since there is evidence that the potential for confusion exists for hearing participants, it is worth pursuing an examination of source attribution in both ASL and English utterances in future research.

Source attribution is a category of interpreter-generated nonrendition that is essential to the relaying of interactive discourse. Interpreters can use a variety of linguistic strategies to attribute source. Moreover, interpreters sometimes do not provide attribution of source at all. The inclusion or exclusion of such information has the potential to influence the comprehensibility of the interactive discourse. Thus, further investigation of various strategies for providing source information, and when such information is and is not provided, could assist in elucidating the kinds of influences interpreters have on interactive discourse.

Repetition

Repetition serves as a second function of interpreter nonrenditions. In the mock medical interview, there is one example of a repetition resulting from an overlap in the dialogue that can be found. The interpreter generates a repetition of her English rendition, although the original author does not. In the actual medical interview, four occurrences of repetitions can be found. Of these, one is the result of an overlap in the discourse.

Just prior to the following example, the mother has asked the doctor if her son's lungs are clear. The doctor provides an answer, during which the mother attempts to initiate a turn:

Example 4.14

177

M:

D: Yeah he may cough, but his lungs are clear. I mean =

N:

C:

I:

I: NO PRO.3 MAYBE COUGH BUT LUNGS TRUE =

178

M:

D: = He'll cough and sound like there's something there an- it has nothing more to do than
     there's stuff =

N:

C:

I:

I: = CLEAR MAYBE COUGH SOUND SAME BUT =

179

M: BEC- BECAUSE PRO.1 HUSBAND #WAS SAY THAT PRO.3 YEL-

D: = draining down from his nose and his ears if we clear up the ears we'll clear up the cough.

N:

C:

I:

I: = JUST DRIP-FROM-EAR FROM EARS NOSE #IF #IF CLEAR EARS BUT- COUGH =

180

M: OH-I-SEE BECAUSE PRO.1 HUSBAND #WAS SAY =

D:

N:

C:

I: 'Cause my husband was saying that =

I: = FUTURE CLEAR SAME

The doctor answers the question in the first line, "Yeah, he may cough, but his lungs are clear." The answer is followed by a more detailed explanation. During this explanation, the mother begins to sign BECAUSE while gazing at the interpreter. The mother then shifts her gaze to the doctor and begins her utterance. Whether or not the doctor is aware of the attempted interruption, he pauses slightly, but does not yield his turn. He adds the conditional "if we clear up the ears we'll clear up the cough." The interpreter pauses and appears ready to begin her English interpretation of the mother's comment when the doctor utters this conditional statement. The interpreter then signs #IF, and as the mother shifts her gaze back to the interpreter, the interpreter repeats the #IF and continues on with her rendition. This brief repetition is a result of the overlapping dialogue. The overlap that occurs in this example is an overlap between the interpreter and the mother. It is conceivable that neither the doctor nor the nurse are aware of the overlap in the ASL discourse. Because interpreters must follow somewhat behind the original utterances in order to understand and then render them, the mother might begin her turn as an overlap with the interpreter's utterance in hope of making up for the lag in time and effectively gaining the floor. The interpreter's repetition effectively regains the Deaf participant's eye gaze in order to allow for rendering of the doctor's utterance. Although this example of repetition is an interpreter-generated nonrendition (the doctor does not repeat this part of his original) related to the relaying of an utterance, it clearly bears a relationship to the management of the interaction and the talking and yielding of turns. For an in-depth discussion of an interpreter's strategies for managing turns in an interpreted encounter see Roy (1989a).

The second type of repetition is related to the redoing of a rendition. This can be seen in the following example, in which the doctor is eliciting detailed information about the child's symptoms:

Example 4.15

52

M:

D: Okay, how many times did he vomit from the time it started?

N:

C:

I:

I: #OK HOW- MANY- HOW OFTEN VOMIT. START SICK, VOMIT, HOW OFTEN?

In her original rendition of the doctor's utterance, the interpreter produces a transliteration or contact variety in a manner consistent with the code choices made by the Deaf participant. However, the code choice causes a problem in the production of a rendition. The interpreter begins her first rendition by signing HOW MANY, which is a direct lexical transliteration of the doctor's original phrase in English, "How many . . ." However, as the doctor continues his utterance, adding the word "times" to the phrase "How many times . . . ," the interpreter initiates a repair. She changes her utterance to HOW OFTEN VOMIT, which is a direct translation of the doctor's utterance up to that point. Finally, as the doctor completes his utterance with a reference to time, "from the time it started," the interpreter repeats her rendition.

In ASL, time-related events are generally uttered in the sequence in which they occur. In addition, ASL makes use of a spatial time line in which a signer can move forward to show the passage of time (cf. Friedman 1975; Baker and Cokely 1980; Winston 1991). The interpreter has the option to continue with her contact variety/transliteration, or to redo the entire rendition in order to incorporate the ASL-appropriate spatial and sequential markers of time. She opts for the latter, signing START SICK, VOMIT, HOW OFTEN? while shifting her body from a backward lean to a forward lean. Thus, this repetition is the result of the redoing of a rendition. It has been categorized as a nonrendition because the primary author's utterance did not include such a repetition.

Although there are a limited number of repetitions in the data, it is interesting to note the two types of repetitions that do occur. The first example of repetition is due to overlap. Roy has described the interpreter's role with regard to overlaps and other aspects of turn-taking as one in which the interpreter is not a neutral conduit providing access between two members of a dyad, but rather that "the interpreter is an active member of interpreted conversations" (1989a, 263). Similarly, when the interpreter redoes a rendition in order to code-switch, this repetition demonstrates that the interpreter, and not the original author of the utterance, is making this conversational choice.

Requests for Clarification

The third type of relaying identified in the professional interpreter's nonrenditions involves requests for clarification. The interpreter makes three such requests: once to the nurse, once to the doctor, and once to the mother. There are two reasons why the interpreter makes such requests—distractions and lack of relevant background knowledge.

There is evidence that the interpreter frames the interview, in part, as a research study. Her schema for this frame causes her to respond differently to the researcher's utterances than to the utterances of the other participants. That is, when the researcher addresses the interpreter during the medical interview, the interpreter does not respond until the nurse leaves the room. Nevertheless, when the researcher distracts the interpreter from the task of interpreting, she misses something that the nurse is saying and is unable to render that:

Example 4.16

21

M: (points left to interpreter)

D:

N: = boys- a hundred boys his age. As far as weight and height are concerned.

C:

I:

I: = COMPARE (..?..)   LIST: (?) MEASURE (?) (looks left)

22

M:

D:

N: He's off the chart for his weight (laughs). He's off the chart, he's - he's way at- at uh, =

C:

I: (to nurse) Pardon?

I: PRO.3 FINISH (?) TOOK-OFF

In this example, the interpreter gazes to the left, toward the researcher, at the point when the researcher (off-camera) produces an

ASL utterance. Rather than interpreting the utterance, or regulating the overlap, the interpreter pauses momentarily and then asks the nurse to repeat, when she says, "Pardon?" This is the only point at which the interpreter appears to be distracted in this manner.

The second request for clarification arises from the interpreter's need to either obtain additional background information or to compensate for gaps in her knowledge. In the following example, the mother is explaining to the doctor that she will get her son's records from another local pediatric center where she has taken her son in the past:

Example 4.17

138

M: YES (+ voice) PRO.1 FUTURE GET #IT =

D: It would be nice to have, uh, some of that history because I mean I can't -

N:

C:

I: = infection, that he had.   Yeah, =

I: FUTURE NICE ABLE HAVE SOME LIST HISTORY

139

M: = FROM INDEX (rt) + POSS.1 DOCTOR PRO.1 GET CL:G FROM #GT UNIVERSITY =

D:

N:

C:

I: = I will get it- I'll get from my other doctor. I have an appointment - =

I:

140

M: = P-E-D-   (to interpreter) #GT UNIVERSITY P-E-D-I-A-T-R-I-C CENTER INDEX (rt)=

D: All right =

N:

C:

I: = (**head tilt left**) (head nods) from Georgetown uh, the pediatric center there?

I:

In this example, the mother, who grew up locally, uses a local sign for the name of the organization, #GT. However, the interpreter is not from the local area, and so is not familiar with the local sign and its referent. She requests clarification by tilting her head slightly to the left, at which time the mother shifts her gaze to the interpreter and responds to the request. The interpreter is able to complete the sentence after the repetition, although her English rendition of the name of the organization is not quite the same as the English one would hear from a local resident, due to her omission of the word "University." Because the background knowledge of the signer and the interpreter are not identical, the interpreter requested clarification. This negotiation led to a successful rendition of the mother's original utterance.

A similar circumstance occurs in the following example in which the doctor is giving the mother a diagnosis of the child's problem:

Example 4.18

161

M:

D: So . . . Um . . .   P.E. stands for physal- physical exam

N:

C:

I:

I: = TO BREATHE THROUGH NOSE   P-E MEAN PHYSICAL SEARCH (body)=

162

M:

D: = he has **bilateral otitis,**   **bilateral, both sides- both ears,** otitis immediate- the right =

N:

C:

I: **(to doctor) he has what?**

I: PRO.3 HAVE   B-I-L-A-T-E-R-A-L ʙᴏᴛʜ ᴇᴀʀs (two hands) O-T-I-T-I-S =

163

M:

D: = is a little worse than the left,   and I'm putting him on (?) . . . that's a penicillin =

N:

C:

I:

I: = ʀɪɢʜᴛ ʟɪᴛᴛʟᴇ ᴡᴏʀsᴇ ᴛʜᴀɴ ʟᴇꜰᴛ   PRO.1 ɢɪᴠᴇ-ᴛᴏ (baby)   A-U-G-M-E-N-T-A-I-N =

The doctor indicates that the child has "bilateral otitis." This condition appears to be unfamiliar to the interpreter, who requests clarification from the doctor: "He has what?" It is possible that the interpreter is familiar with the condition, but has simply not heard what the doctor said. However, the doctor appears to treat the request as if it is related to background knowledge, and in his response he defines the terms in an attempt to clarify them, as in "bilateral, both sides, both ears."

Whether the mother is familiar with this condition does not become clear. If the interpreter had provided an accurate rendition to the mother, three possible outcomes might have resulted. First, the mother might have understood and allowed the interaction to continue. Second, the mother might not have understood, yet might have, for some reason, decided not to comment. Third, the mother might not have understood and requested clarification herself. Although it is impossible to know what might have happened, it seems clear that the interpreter, who makes a legitimate request for clarification, has had an impact on the outcome of this portion of the interaction.

The interpreter requests clarification from each of the participants in the interview. One reason for requesting clarification is due
to distractions from what the interpreter is focused on as the task at
hand. A second reason for requesting clarification is to assist in understanding an utterance that contains information that might be familiar to the other participant(s), but that is new to the interpreter.
Both of these causes for clarification requests are inherent to the
task of interpreting. That is, interpreters can never have background
knowledge that is identical to that of any one or all of the participants. In addition, while one can attempt to limit distractions, it
would be impossible to eliminate the potential for distractions (e.g.,
phones ringing, rainstorms, failing books or chairs, and so forth).
Thus, the particular context of a given interaction will have an impact on all the participants, including the interpreter. Likewise, all
the participants, including the interpreter, will have an impact on
the situated interaction.

Summary

Both source attribution and repetition occur in the actual medical
interview, just as they are identifiable functions of the interpreter's
footings in the mock medical interview. In addition, the professional
interpreter's footings include requests for clarification resulting
from distractions of the interpreter or distinctions between the interpreter's and the other participants' background knowledge. The
latter category, like source attribution, indicates that interpreters
cannot be neutral in the sense of simply rendering decontextualized
utterances. As Seleskovitch (1978) has said of spoken language conference interpreters, an interpreter must be able to understand in order to interpret.

Interactional Management

In the actual medical interview, there are nineteen interpreter-
generated nonrenditions that pertain to interactional management.
Although the actual medical encounter does not contain any introductions, as did the mock interview, both responses to questions and

Table 4.6   Occurrences of Interactional Management in Actual
Medical Interview

	N	Responses to Questions (%)	Interference (%)	Summonses (%)
Number of Occurrences	19	1 (5.3%)	6 (31.6%)	12 (63.1%)

interference occur in the data. Summonses represent an additional
function that did not occur in the mock case but does occur in the
actual medical interview (see table 4.6).

Responses to Questions
Like the student interpreter, the professional interpreter generally
does not respond to questions directed at her during the course of the
medical interview. In the actual medical encounter, the doctor and
nurse address questions to the interpreter, but the Deaf participant
does not. In addition, the hearing researcher addresses a question to
the interpreter. The latter of these is the only question that the interpreter responds to in the entire interview.

Throughout the encounter, the doctor and nurse direct numerous questions to the interpreter. Many of these are questions for
which the mother has the answers. These types of questions take a
form in which the mother is talked *about* rather than talked *to*. An
example of this can be seen in line 10 below:

Example 4.19

10

Nurse: Does she have his shot records?

The interpreter merely relays, rather than redirects, these types of
questions. They are then answered by the mother and rendered by the

interpreter as a direct response. This is noteworthy because this is what the student interpreter appeared to be striving toward in the mock medical interview. In that case, however, the Deaf person did not always respond. In at least one example in the mock medical interview, this left an unfilled slot in a question-answer adjacency pair.

Because the questions from the doctor and nurse in the actual medical interview are generally answered by the mother, there appear to be no major problems in the flow of the interaction. Nevertheless, it is not clear whether the doctor and nurse understand who is the principal for the interpreter's utterances. In the earlier example of the doctor requesting clarification regarding the referent of a first-person pronoun, the interpreter does not generate a response for which she is the principal. However, since she is authoring the mother's discourse as constructed dialogue, using first person to refer to the mother, the doctor obtains the information he needs without further confusion. The example below begins with the mother's response to the doctor's question: "You tried or she tried?" The mother is explaining the fact that she herself is the principal of the interpreter's utterances:

Example 4.20

57

M: = LET PRO.1 EXPLAIN. WHEN INTERPRETER TRUE INTERPRET, PRO.3 WILL =

D:

N:

C:

I: = Now let me explain. When the interpreter is interpreting, she will be speaking =

I:

58

M: = BE TALK A-S I-F PRO.3 NOT I-N ROOM PRO.3. TALK FOR PRO.1, #SO (?off screen) =

D: (chuckles)   Okay, gotcha.

N:

C:

I: = as if, she's not in the room.   She's speaking for me.   So, if it =

I:

59

M: = CONFUSE TRUE TALK PRO.1, A-S I-F PRO.3 PRO.1

D: I'm just interested in the pronoun, that's all.

N:

C:

I: = confuses you, the interpreter's really speaking as if-

I: PRO.1 (REALLY) INTEREST =

60

M: #OK PRO.1

D: You're not taking care =

N:

C: (cries)

I:

I: = WORD "I" (i on chest) PRO.3 (left hand) I (i on chest)

61

M: NO PRO.1 RECENT MEET- (interpreter) #HER FIRST TIME =

D: = of him, you're just interpreting.

N:

C: (crying continues)

I: I just met =

I: NOT PRO.1, PRO.1 NOT TAKE-CARE -

62

M: = NOW.

D: okay   I've been in practice thirty-five years, I've =

N:				
C:				(screams then crying stops)
I:	= her for the first time today, so			
I:		#OK	PRO. 1 . . .	PRO.1 WORK++ =

In line 60, the doctor directs another question to the interpreter: "You're not taking care of him, you're just interpreting." Once again, the interpreter does not respond to the question. As the mother responds that she has only just met the interpreter for the first time, the interpreter's rendering "I just met her for the first time today, so," likely answers the doctor's question for the wrong reason. That is, the referent for the interpreter's first-person pronoun is the mother, not the interpreter. Moreover, the interpreter is referring to herself in the third person, with "her." It is likely that the doctor mistakenly assumes that the interpreter is referring to herself in the first person, and that the third-person pronoun refers to the mother. Because the interpreter and the Deaf participant are the same gender, there is no way to know for certain who the intended referents for these pronouns are. Nevertheless, on the basis of the interpreter's eye gaze and the content of the mother's recent utterance, it seems likely that the interpreter did not generate the response. Fortunately, the response provided the doctor with accurate information, regardless of whether or not he was entirely clear about who originated it.

The only time that the interpreter actually answers a question is when the researcher asks her if she can move into view of the video camera. The interpreter waits to respond until a break in the interpreted encounter frame, when the nurse leaves the room:

Example 4.21

32	
M:	
D:	
N:	Doctor should be in in just a few minutes (exits)
C:	

I: (to researcher behind camera) **Wha'd you say?**

I: DOCTOR COME FEW MINUTE

33

M: FINE WHERE?

D:

N:

C:

I: (moves so visible) **How's this? (nods) If we can rid of this chair, 'cause the doctor's not** =

I: (arms moving but signs not visible)

34

M: TEND SIT INDEX (to another seat)   (shakes head)

D:

N:

C:

I: = **gonna sit in it.**

I: **(to mother)** PRO.2 SIT (IN CHAIR)?

35

M: U-N-L-E-S-S #DR WANT PRO.1 HOLD PRO.3 (to baby) (shrugs)

D:

N:

C:

I: **If we can- I'll just (?)**

I: MOVE

36

M: PRO.2 STAR! SAME FATHER =

D:

N:

C: (sees video camera)

I: (moves chair) **Better**   (laughs)

I: BETTER

The interpreter responds by complying with the researcher's request. The interpreter moves and asks, "How's this?" When the move is not sufficient to resolve the logistical problem, the interpreter asks the mother if she will use one of the two chairs in the room, and then moves it out of the way in order to situate herself such that she can be seen by both the mother and the camera.

Although numerous questions are directed to the interpreter in the actual medical interview, her only response is directed to the researcher and occurs during an out-of-frame period of the interview. Her lack of responses to the doctor and nurse, unlike the student interpreter's nonresponses, do not include explanations about the current circumstance. However, whether or not the professional interpreter would include such explanations if the Deaf participant did not intervene with responses and explanations is not clear from this data. This would be an interesting area for future research. Since the Deaf participant does not direct any questions to the professional interpreter, it is also not clear how the interpreter would respond in such a situation. This also would be another area for additional research. It is worth noting, however, that the Deaf participant in the mock interview directed utterances to the interpreter only during frame breaks (when the doctor left the room). The Deaf participant in the actual interview used this time to communicate with the researcher, who is of relatively long acquaintance, rather than to the newly met interpreter. If the researcher had not been present, it is conceivable that the Deaf participant might have interacted with the interpreter on a different footing during these out-of-frame periods. Perhaps a larger corpus of data and different videotaping circumstances would allow for such interaction to be caught on videotape.

Interference

Interference, as described with regard to the mock interview, refers to footing shifts that result from the physical environment. Although no blatant environmental interferences occur, two examples of interference are responsible for the professional interpreter's non-renditions. One of these examples is the result of the physical presence of the camera and researcher, while the other results from the use of an underarm thermometer in an encounter that involves ASL-English interpretation.

The presence of the researcher and camera add an additional logistical burden to the interpreter. While ASL-English interpreters must consider numerous logistical issues in terms of both visual and auditory accessibility (cf. Frishberg 1990), the researcher puts an additional demand on these logistical considerations by requesting that the interpreter remain in view of the video camera. The small size of the examination room and the need to see participants at a clear angle (allowing for readability of manual and nonmanual linguistic information) necessitated such a request. All the interpreter's nonrenditions that address the logistical issues related to the presence of the camera are the result of this interference.

The second example of interference occurs when the nurse attempts to take the child's temperature using an underarm thermometer. In this example, the mother is watching the interpreter's renditions, holding her son, attempting to hold his arm down so that the thermometer remains in place, and also conversing with the nurse. Because the mother uses her hands to communicate, the attempt to hold her son and his thermometer at the same time seems analogous to a hearing English speaker attempting to converse with a dentist with the dental instruments in his or her mouth:

Example 4.22

25

M: ALWAYS B-E-E-N THAT W-A-Y

D:

N: And he's just below the ninetieth for his length but he's way off the chart for his weight.

C:

I:

I: (?) UNDER   (?)   #TH MEASURE

26
M:
D:
N: Okay, did that stop =
C:
I:
I: WEIGHT TOOK-OFF **LOOK-AT** (baby's underarm thermometer)

27
M: I D-O I-N R-E-A-R INDEX
D:
N: = beeping? No . . . this is gonna be impossible.   (?)
C:
I:
I: INDEX IMPOSSIBLE   WELL #OK

28
M: EASIER FINISH EASIER   #IF PRO.1 =
D:
N: (laughs) We try to get 'em not too excited before . . . they see the doctor.
C:
I: I do it in his rear.
I: WE TRY- DON'T-WANT OR EXCITE BEFORE-

The interpreter is rendering the nurse's report regarding the child's weight. At the end of this rendition, the interpreter generates a non-rendition, "LOOK-AT (baby's underarm thermometer)," directing the mother to look at the thermometer, which is slipping out from under the child's arm. Information about the physical environment can be considered an interference to the existing footing. Nevertheless, in this case the interpreter is providing information about the physical environment that might not otherwise be noticed by the mother, who cannot look in two places at the same time.

Two examples of interference occur in the actual medical interview. In the first example, the presence of the researcher and video camera are responsible for the shift in the interpreter's footing to a self-generated nonrendition. In the second example, it is the fact that the Deaf participant might not notice relevant aspects of the physical environment while maintaining eye contact with the interpreter. In future research it would be interesting to determine the extent to which interpreters provide certain contextual information to Deaf participants.

Summonses

The third type of interactional management identified in the actual interview is a type of nonrendition that did not occur in the mock medical interview. Summonses, or attention-getting strategies, comprise twelve of the interpreter's twenty-nine nonrenditions. In the discussion of source attribution it became clear that information regarding the identity and location of the source (or original author) of an utterance is not necessarily accessible to the other participants without additional information being provided by the interpreter. An adjunct to this is whether or not the participants know when an interlocutor begins an utterance.

Hearing English speakers may or may not be aware that signing has originated from the interpreter or the Deaf participant, but once the interpreter begins to speak, they know that an utterance is beginning. Conversely, for a Deaf participant, presence in the room is not enough to provide information that someone is signing an utterance. The issue of utterance accessibility becomes relevant with regard to the channel in which the message is being sent. If it is sent through the visual channel, the receiver's eyes must be directed at, and within the discriminatory range of, the source of the visible message. If it is sent through the acoustic channel, the ears of the receiver must simply be within the discriminatory range of the acoustic message source. Thus, it is essential that the Deaf interlocutor receive a visual cue to attend to the upcoming discourse (cf. Baker 1977; Haas, Fleetwood, and Ernest 1995).

Baker (1977) analyzes this phenomenon in ASL discourse and identifies three types of "initiation regulators," or summonses, that serve this function: indexing, touching the addressee, or waving a hand in front of him or her. In addition, Mather (1994) examines the attention-getting strategies of Deaf native signers with Deaf toddlers. One of the strategies that the Deaf adults use is what Mather terms "eye-level gaze" or EL-GAZE. When a Deaf child is engaged in an activity, the Deaf adult moves into the child's line of vision in order to begin signing to the child. In the interpreted medical encounter, indexing occurs two times, touching occurs one time, hand waving occurs eight times, and EL-GAZE occurs one time. The interpreter produces a total of twelve summonses in the data.

An example of both indexing and EL-GAZE can be seen in the following example. At this point in the interview the doctor is prescribing treatment to help curtail the child's vomiting. The mother is trying to indicate that she has resolved that part of her son's illness, and that he is no longer experiencing this particular symptom. The interpreter, obviously unable to manage two linguistic messages simultaneously, is shifting between renderings of the doctor's and the mother's utterances so that while neither participant gets it all, both participants get some semblance of the overlapping discourse:

Example 4.23

144

M:

D: ah- when a- when a baby is vomiting, first of all, ah, we immediate- the =

N:

C:

I:

I: BABY VOMIT FIRST, (palms out) BABY VOMIT =

145

M:

D: = treatment of- of uh vomiting, like with diarrhea is the diet. Uh, and, the diet, basically =

N:

C: (starts crying)

I:

I: = DO-DO? TO HELP-TO (baby) VOMIT SAME WITH DIARRHEA SAME D-I-E-T FOOD =

146

M: (head forward, brows raised)

D: = with vomiting the diet is small quantities, of clear liquids, frequently. =

N:

C:

I:

I: = IMPORTANT WHAT EAT IMPORTANT WITH VOMIT MUST PROVIDE =

147

M: **PRO.1-**   **(TO DOCTOR) PRO.1 GIVE WATER-**

D: = So that you don't fill his,   stomach up,   and then it'll bring it up. =

N:

C:

I:

I: = SMALL-AMOUNT CLEAR L-I-Q-U-I-D-S HOLD PROVIDE+ OFTEN PRO.2 NOT =

148

M:

D: = Uh, in just little, bits, =

N:

C:

I:

I: = FILL-TO-CHEST DON'T-WANT VOMIT (inflected, from abdomen) AGAIN

149

M: (to doctor) WATER VOMIT T-H-A-T U-P =

D: = frequently.   And uh,   Okay, better to give him, uh =

N:

C:

I: **I've been giving him water** . . . and he threw that up, too: =

I: = LITTLE+ + BUT OFTEN

150

M: = (head shake) THAT- PRO.3 NOT VOMIT UP-TO-NOW WEDNESDAY.   PRO.1 TRY THAT =

D: =   either   Pediolite or   Gatorade? =

N:

C:

I:

I: **INDEX (held up)** EITHER THAT #OR PROVIDE P-E-D-I-O-L-I-T-E AND =

151

M: = NOT WORK.   FINISH D-I SAME D-I-D I-N-F-A-N-T-I-L

D: = uh, she could use either one, Gatorade is over age twelve months Gatorade is- =

N:

C:

I: I've already tried those and he threw that up.

I: = **G-A-T-O-R- (shift into mom's view)** G-A-T-O-R-A-D-E FINISH

152

M: PRO.3 (head shake) B-E-E-N VOMIT UP-TO-NOW LAST-WEEK WEDNESDAY

D: = in little quantities frequently, little quantities. Uh, and um,

N:

C:

I: He hasn't been throwing up =

I: LITTLE+ + OFTEN

153

M: = #SO PRO.1 NOT T-O-O CONCERN ABOUT THAT ANY MORE

D: okay so-   okay   okay

N:

C:

I: = since last Wednesday, now, so: I'm not too concerned about that anymore.

I: #OK++

In line 147 the mother attempts to initiate a turn. The interpreter retains the mother's content, and renders it in line 149, by completing a part of the doctor's utterance and talking the floor during the doctor's moment of hesitation, "And uh,-." The doctor quickly resumes his turn while the mother continues her explanation. Since the mother is not gazing at the interpreter during her utterance, she cannot know that the doctor has resumed unless she is summoned by the interpreter in order to access the rendition of the doctor's talk. It is worth noting here that the interpreter could have yielded the turn to the mother, continuing to render the mother's utterance into English (and possibly overlapping with the doctor's talk). Roy (1989a) finds that an interpreter interpreting in an academic meeting frequently yields turns to the hearing professor rather than to the Deaf student, and suggests that the relative status of the interlocutor's social roles might be the rationale behind such a choice. If true, a similar consideration could be at work here. In line 150 the interpreter holds up her hand, index finger extended, to get the mother's attention and then begins to render the doctor's portion of the overlapping dialogue. The mother watches the interpreter's rendition, but when mention is made of "Pediolite" the mother immediately explains that she tried the doctor's suggestion before and it was ineffective. The mother's gaze leaves the interpreter after she renders the doctor's first suggestion (Pediolite), but before she renders the second suggestion (Gatorade). Once again, the mother cannot know that the doctor has made a second suggestion, unless she is looking when the interpreter renders it. In line 151 the interpreter, noticing the lack of eye gaze, shifts into the mother's line of vision (EL-GAZE) as she resumes her rendition of the second item in the doctor's list, "G-A-T-O-R- . . . G-A-T-O-R-A-D-E." It is interesting to note that this example includes both indexing and EL-GAZE within a short span of discourse. It would be interesting to determine how much the various attention-getting strategies vary in degree, intensity, or politeness. This question is also relevant to the next example, which induces occurrences of both touching and hand waving.

In the following example (seen in parts in examples 3.14 and 3.15) the doctor interrupts the interpreter's rendition and the mother's original utterance in order to request clarification of the referent of a first-person pronoun:

Example 4.24

52

M: PRO.3 START VOMIT =

D: = times did he vomit from the time it started.

N:

C:

I:

I: = MANY- HOW OFTEN VOMIT. START SICK, VOMIT, HOW OFTEN?

53

M: = TUESDAY NIGHT, FINISH BY WEDNESDAY AFTERNOON . . . FINISH

D: Okay.

N:

C:

I: He started vomiting Tuesday night, and finished Wednesday late afternoon.

I: #OK

54

M: VOMIT EVERY TIME PRO.1 TRY GIVE PRO.3 (neutral) SOMETHING VOMIT . . . #SO =

D: And the fever's -

N:

C:

I: And he threw up, um, **and every time he threw up I tried to give him something,** so: =

I:

55

M: = PRO.1 GIVE-UP . . .   E-V-E-N L-I-Q-U-I-D-S   PRO.1

D: **You (points to interpreter) tried or she (points to mother) tried?**

N:

C:

I: = I don't know: I- (looks at doctor) I tried =

I: (waves)

56

M: = PRO.1 + + (glances to interpreter) NO (taps doctor's arm) PRO.3 INTERPRETER

D:

N:

C:

I: = to give him liquids too.

I: (taps mother's knee) PRO.1 TRY OR PRO.2 TRY?

As the interpreter finishes rendering the mother's utterance, she also waves for the mother's attention in order to inform her that the doctor has produced an utterance. At this point, the mother has apparently read the doctor's lips, and in line 55 she indicates that it is she, the mother, who is the child's caretaker. The interpreter does not see the mother sign her response to the doctor's not yet rendered question. Both the mother and the interpreter glance back and forth between each other and the doctor, as the mother begins her utterance. The interpreter, intent on rendering the doctor's question, first waves for the mother's attention and then taps her on the knee. Interestingly, the mother tries to initiate an explanation two times before the interpreter is able to get her attention long enough to render the doctor's request. The mother even touches the doctor's arm and begins a third attempt at explanation by signing to him directly. Unfortunately, the doctor is not visible on the screen at this point in the data. Therefore, there is no way to know at whom he is gazing or what his response is to the mother's touch. In any case, however, he does not respond verbally. At this point the interpreter touches the mother's knee, and as the interpreter renders the doctor's request for clarification, the mother briefly glances at the interpreter, then gazes down and begins her fourth (and successfully rendered) attempt to respond.

The doctor's request, which is an other-initiation of a self-repair (Schegloff, Jefferson, and Sacks 1977), causes some disruption for the mother and the interpreter. Both the mother and the interpreter recognize the request for a repair. However, the doctor has addressed this request to the interpreter, as the author of the English utterance, including the pronoun in question. The interpreter is not the principal of the utterance, however. The mother and interpreter both exhibit increased eye gaze shifts, and there is a negotiation of turns between them while the doctor waits for a response. After 6.4 seconds, the interpreter and the mother resolve their disruption and the mother begins the repair that is rendered by the interpreter. The fact that the doctor is referring to the English discourse between himself and the interpreter, and that the interpreter and the mother negotiate in ASL the handling of the response, indicates that the interpreted encounter does not represent a single dyad between the mother and the doctor. Moreover, the indication here is that the interpreted encounter does not represent triadic discourse either. This is a critical issue regarding the interpreter's influence on the interactive discourse and will be addressed in greater depth in chapter 5.

In both of the previous examples there are two types of summonses within close proximity to one another. In future research, it would be interesting to investigate whether or not the four types of attention-getting devices have different interactional functions. It is also noteworthy that while there is such a high occurrence of summonses among the interpreter's nonrenditions in the actual medical interview, there are no occurrences of such devices in the mock medical interview. One reason for this could be that the mock interview is specifically designed for the purpose of interpreting, with all three participants facing one another and intent on the interpreted encounter frame. An additional explanation could be that there are no children present in the mock interview. In the actual interview, the Deaf interlocutor is responsible for and concerned about her young son, who is crying for much of the encounter. When the child needs her attention, she looks away from the interpreter, thus providing more opportunities for the interpreter to summon her. Nevertheless, this is not the only reason for a summons. The mother attempts to initiate a turn and the interpreter summons her in order to finish a rendition of the doctor's utterance. Regardless of the causes for a summons, if the interpreter omitted it, the mother would unknowingly miss information. Clearly, these nonrenditions are critical to the management of the ASL-English interpreted interaction.

Like the student interpreter, the professional interpreter's footing types include those related to the task of managing the interaction. Two categories of these footing types, responses to questions and interference, are found in both the actual and the mock medical interviews. An additional type of footing found in the actual medical interview is the interpreter's use of summonses. Where summonses provide information that is necessary when the Deaf participant is not gazing at the interpreter, interference provides environmental information for the Deaf participant who is gazing at the interpreter. Thus, these two footings both indicate that certain paralinguistic or contextual information is conveyed to the Deaf participant by the professional interpreter. The absence of responses to questions directed to the interpreter in the actual medical interview is also notable in that the student interpreter attempts the same strategy somewhat unsuccessfully where the professional interpreter succeeds. It seems that a major difference in these results originates in the schema and behavior exhibited by another participant, in this case the Deaf participant. Because the Deaf participant responds to the questions posed by the medical practitioners, and because explanations regarding the interpreter's footing are provided by the Deaf participant, the interaction is able to proceed relatively smoothly. Through examination of a larger corpus of data, it would be interesting to identify various strategies used by different participants and the effect they have on interpreters' strategies for interactional management.

*Relayings and Interactional Management in the Actual
Medical Interview*

As in the case of the mock interview, both the existence and the variety of the nonrenditions and the footings they represent indicate that the interpreter does influence interpreted interactive discourse. Nevertheless, the function of many of the footings is related to the goal of providing access to aspects of the interaction that would be unknown to one or another of the participants if the interpreter merely rendered utterances. This supports Roy's contention that interpreters are not merely conduits providing access to linguistic communication between interactional partners (1989a). Nevertheless, it is interesting to note that, as in the mock case, approximately three-quarters of the interpreter's nonrenditions are directed to the Deaf participant only. Does this finding indicate that these interpreters are not impartial in the provision of their services? If interpreters demonstrate a partiality for one or another participant (e.g., Deaf over hearing), what kind of influence does this have on the interaction and the participants' perceptions of interpreted encounters? The next section will address the first of these issues by providing a comparison of the two cases under examination. The latter question will be addressed in chapter 5.

Comparison of Footing Types in the Two Cases of Interpreted Encounters

Examination of the code used in the interpreter-generated nonrenditions indicates that both the student and the professional interpreter directed a majority of nonrenditions to the Deaf participant in each encounter (see table 4.7). In addition, there is a smaller but notable difference in the occurrence of spoken only and simultaneously signed and spoken utterances. Because the choice of one or another language code necessarily ratifies some participants and denies access to others, it might appear on the surface that simultaneously produced utterances allow for ratification of all participants. For an interpreter striving toward neutrality, this would appear to be a potentially effective strategy, and in fact, is a strategy used by the student interpreter on various occasions within the mock interview.

Participation Frameworks

Table 4.7   Comparison of Occurrences of Interpreter-
Generated Nonrenditions in Mock and Actual Interviews

	Mock Medical Interview	Actual Medical Interview	Combined Total Occurrences
Signed and Spoken	3 (20.0%)	3 (10.3%)	6 (13.6%)
Spoken Only	1 (6.7%)	4 (13.8%)	5 (11.4%)
Signed Only	11 (73.3%)	22 (75.9%)	33 (75.0%)
Total *N*	15	29	44

Nevertheless, research has indicated that although signed and spoken languages appear to be simultaneously producible as a result of their distinct media of articulation (visual and acoustic), their diverse linguistic structures do not allow for effective simultaneous production (see Johnson, Liddell, and Erting 1989; Johnson and Erting 1989). Thus, it is important to note that the student interpreter produced a higher ratio of simultaneously signed and spoken utterances (20 percent) than the professional interpreter (10.3 percent). Further, the student interpreter's use of simultaneous code choices tended to result in utterances with flawed and potentially confusing linguistic form. Moreover, the professional interpreter's use of simultaneously signed and spoken utterances had an apparently different function from those of the student interpreter. The professional interpreter never produced such utterances in the presence of the hearing participants who were not fluent in ASL. Thus, on the basis of these two cases, the simultaneously signed and spoken utterances seem to be problematic for the student interpreter and not employed by the professional as a strategy for ratifying all participants at the same time.

In terms of utterances produced only in spoken English, the professional interpreter apparently produces a higher ratio (13.8 percent) than the student interpreter (6.7 percent). However, only two of the four spoken utterances occur with the doctor and/or nurse present in the room. The other two are directed at the hearing researcher during a frame break. Therefore, the professional interpreter produced just two spoken-only utterances of the twenty-nine interpreter-generated nonrenditions found within the context of the medical interview itself (6.9 percent). Based on this comparison, both interpreters produced a comparable percentage of spoken-only utterances. This percentage, less than one-eighth of all the interpreter-generated nonrenditions combined, is quite low. The spoken-only utterances consisted solely of relayings (requests for clarification on the part of the professional interpreter, and a repetition on the part of the student interpreter). This is inconsistent with the function of the signed-only utterances.

The greatest proportion of interpreter-generated nonrenditions are signed only. Both interpreters produced approximately three quarters of their utterances as signed only. Like the spoken utterances, these included relayings (requests for clarification and repetitions). Unlike the utterances addressed to hearing participants, the utterances addressed to the Deaf participants consist of all six types of footings identified in the data, as well as both relaying and interactional management functions. Some of these footing types are applicable only to the Deaf participants. For instance, a summons can serve a unique function in ASL. Hearing participants know that when the interpreter produces a spoken utterance, there is information to which they can attend, whereas Deaf participants who are not gazing at the interpreter will not know unless the interpreter informs them visually.

Other types of footing are not so language- or modality-specific. For example, without clarification from the interpreter, source attribution can be equally confusing to both hearing and Deaf participants. If the interpreter provides more of this type of information to Deaf participants, leaving hearing participants confused, such potentially favorable partiality toward Deaf participants would indicate that the interpreters' influence on the interaction is not neutral.

By examining the two cases of interpreters' nonrenditions, it has become clear that the interpreters' choice of code does have an influence on the participation framework of the interactive discourse. Since the interpreter must make a choice that frequently leaves one or another participant as unratified, and since both interpreters generally decide to sign their nonrenditions, there is a tremendous potential for participants to sense partiality on behalf of the Deaf participants. Moreover, since the hearing participants in both encounters demonstrate interpreted-encounter schema that are at odds with the interpreters' schema (possibly because any given Deaf person and any given interpreter encounter interpreted events more frequently than does the average hearing person), it would seem likely that the hearing participants could benefit from information related to the management of the interaction. Nevertheless, examination of the interpreters' code choices indicates that both interpreters prefer two types of interactional alignments: interpreter–Deaf participant and Deaf participant–hearing participant. The interpreters so pointedly attempted to avoid interpreter–hearing participant interactions that they actually avoided responding to interpreter-directed questions from each doctor. The preference for establishing certain participation frameworks is clearly related to the issue of interpreter neutrality.

Comparison of Footing Types: Relayings

In both the mock and actual medical interviews, three types of footings categorized as relayings are identifiable. However, the three types are not identical in each case. The two types of footings that occurred in both cases are source attribution and repetitions. Explanations are produced only by the student interpreter and requests for clarification are produced only by the professional interpreter (see table 4.8). Although both interpreters generated nonrenditions that functioned to attribute the source of rendered utterances, it is interesting to note that almost half of the student's utterances are devoted to this function while less than a third of the professional's utterances serve this function. Because the data indicate that confusion regarding source of a message is a real issue, it is not clear why this footing type comprises such a low percentage of the professional interpreter's utterances. It is possible that the professional

Table 4.8   Comparison of Occurrences of Relayings in Mock
and Actual Interviews

	Mock Medical Interview	Actual Medical Interview	Combined Total Occurrences
Source	4	3	7
Attribution	(44.4%)	(30.0%)	(36.8%)
Explanations	4	0	4
	(44.4%)	(0.0%)	(21.1%)
Repetitions	1	4	5
	(11.1%)	(40.0%)	(26.3%)
Requests for	0	3	3
Clarification	(0.0%)	(30.0%)	(15.8%)
Total N	9	10	19

interpreter, as a native bilingual with Deaf parents is more aware of strategies used by Deaf adults in determining source (e.g., through visual clues). On the other hand, it is possible that source attribution is a strategy that could improve the professional interpreter's interpretation. This is an area that would benefit from future research.

With regard to explanations, it is notable that these also comprise almost half of the student's nonrenditions. This is especially interesting since none of the professional interpreter's nonrenditions consist of explanations. One possible explanation for this is that the professional interpreter is working with a Deaf participant who shares a similar schema regarding the interpreted encounter frame. Thus, explanations regarding the interpreter's presence or role are actually handled by the Deaf participant, rather than the interpreter, in the actual medical encounter. An interesting area for future research would be to identify whether or not participants (Deaf or hearing) who share a schema of the interpreted encounter frame are more likely to provide such explanations than are interpreters. In addition, it would be interesting, in a larger corpus of data, to analyze the types of explanations that are provided by interpreters and whether or not these types of explanations are similar for Deaf and hearing participants.

The largest percentage of relayings produced by the professional interpreter are repetitions. This is interesting because it is the smallest category of footing types displayed by the student interpreter. Nevertheless, both interpreters produced repetitions for similar purposes (e.g., as a result of overlap), though the professional interpreter also produced repetitions as a way of redoing an interpretation of a given rendition. This strategy might be more challenging for a student interpreter who is not natively fluent in both languages. It would be interesting to conduct a longitudinal study of a group of student interpreters to determine whether this type of repetition becomes more prevalent at some point in their professional development.

The final type of relaying found in the data involves requests for clarification. This type of footing comprised nearly a third of the professional interpreter's nonrenditions. However, the student interpreter produced no such requests. One possible explanation for this is that the student, who is coping with the processes of interpretation, does not yet have the ability to make such a request, process the information, and render it while remembering and catching up with the utterances missed in the meantime. A second possibility is that the student interpreter intentionally avoids such a footing, in the same manner that she avoids interacting directly with the hearing participant. A third, and more simple explanation is that the student interpreter does not need information clarified. In fact, since the role play is designed to focus on the interpreting task, there is nothing happening in the room aside from the role play itself. Conversely, in the actual medical encounter, the professional interpreter is coping with a small space, the additional presence of a researcher, and a baby crying almost nonstop throughout the encounter. If this latter reason is the case, it is worth investigating to what extent interpreter education programs offer these realistic contextual factors while training students through role plays. For example, do students practice pediatric examinations in which the needs of a real child are incorporated into the technical redoing?

Many similarities and differences can be identified with regard to relayings between the interpreted mock and actual medical encounters. The findings here indicate that future research regarding these similarities and differences would be worthwhile, not only to better understand the ways in which interpreters influence interactions, but also to determine the relationship between how professional interpreters function and how students of interpreting are being taught to function.

Comparison of Footing Types: Interactional Management

Three types of footings are categorized as interactional management in both the mock and actual medical interviews. As in the findings regarding relayings, the three types are not identical in each case. The two types of footings that occurred in both cases are responses to questions and interference. Introductions are produced only by the student interpreter and summonses are produced only by the professional interpreter (see table 4.9). Unlike the student interpreter, the professional interpreter does not provide any introduction of herself or the reason for her presence. It is not clear why the student provides such an introduction and the professional does not. One explanation is that the student has time to do so, since in the role play the doctor does not bear the realities of the hectic schedule

Table 4.9 Comparison of Occurrences of Interactional Management in Mock and Actual Interviews

	Mock Medical Interview	Actual Medical Interview	Combined Total Occurrences
Introductions	2	0	2
	(33.3%)	(0.0%)	(8.0%)
Responses to Questions	3	1	4
	(50.0%)	(5.3%)	(16.0%)
Interference	1	6	7
	(16.7%)	(31.6%)	(28.0%)
Summonses	0	12	12
	(0.0%)	(63.1%)	(48.0%)
Total N	6	19	25

of a medical practice. Another possibility is that the professional interpreter knows the interpreted encounter has been arranged, in part, by the researcher. Since the researcher is also a professional interpreter, it is conceivable that the informant has assumed that an explanation has already been provided to the Deaf and hearing participants. Future research regarding the presence of such introductions in interpreted encounters, as well as the impact of their presence and absence, would be useful in understanding the ways in which interpreters influence interactive discourse.

Both the student and professional interpreter respond to questions. The student interpreter responds only to questions from the Deaf participant, which occur only during the frame break (no doctor in the room). The professional interpreter also does not provide responses to the hearing medical practitioners. However, the Deaf participant does not address questions to the professional interpreter, so it is not clear whether or not she would respond to the Deaf participant in such an event. Nevertheless, it is interesting to note that the one response generated by the professional interpreter, directed toward the researcher, occurs during a frame break in which no medical practitioners are present. It would be useful, in future studies, to determine whether or not professional interpreters respond to Deaf participants and not to hearing participants. It would also be interesting to study the footing between in-frame and out-of-frame portions of medical interviews.

A second type of footing generated by both interpreters is the result of interference. Although over one-third of the professional interpreter's nonrenditions fit this category, the majority of these are the result of logistical issues presented by the research study. Within the medical interview, there is only one occurrence of such a footing on the part of the professional interpreter. This is comparable to the single occurrence found in the mock interview. The types of interference differ somewhat, however. The utterance resulting from interference on the part of the student is the result of an interference generated by the interpreter herself (touching the doctor's arm while signing). In the case of the actual medical interview, the professional interpreter's utterance is the result of the physical logistics of the situation. That is, whether or not the nurse is aware of it, the Deaf participant must watch the interpreter while the interpreter renders the nurse's discourse. Furthermore, the Deaf participant must use her hands while holding her son and the thermometer under his arm. Perhaps, in an attempt to compensate for the logistical dilemma faced by the mother, the interpreter informs the mother when the thermometer begins to fall from under her child's arm. This type of interference will likely always be a part of ASL-English interpreted encounters. The type of interference generated by the student interpreter is, perhaps, more avoidable.

The final type of footing related to the management of interaction involves summonses. Although the student produced no such utterances, they comprise well over half of the professional interpreter's utterances. Perhaps the student interpreter has no need to summon the Deaf participant because the classroom has been designed for ease of visual accessibility. The Deaf participant is not there out of real concern for his health, but rather to assist in creating an interpreted encounter. All of the participants are seated and facing one another, and there is no need to summon the Deaf participant to regain his attention. An interesting area for further investigation would be to determine whether or not interpreter education programs provide technical redoings that include circumstances requiring summonses. For interpreting students who are not native users of ASL, practice with such a footing could be very beneficial.

There are many interesting areas for further investigation with regard to the footing types that function as interactional management. Perhaps the most outstanding issue of all with regard to this category of footing types is the fact that the majority of them are addressed only to the Deaf participants. Nevertheless, regardless of the recipients of such utterances, the presence of footing types that influence the sequence of the interaction clearly indicates that interpreters are not simple conduits of language.

Implications

An examination of the production format within an interpreted encounter, and the different types of footing established by the interpreter with each interlocutor, demonstrates that the interpreter participates, in some capacity, in the interpreted interaction. The interpreter generates utterances for a variety of purposes, including both relaying information and management of the interactional structure. Because a given footing represents a participant-based frame of an event, the interpreter's footing types provide some insight into the interpreter's negotiation of the Interpreter's Paradox.

The quantitative analysis of interpreter utterances indicates that a relatively small percentage of interpreter utterances are nonrenditions: 13 percent in the mock medical encounter and 80 percent in the actual medical encounter. Comparatively speaking, it is interesting to note the greater percentage of occurrences of nonrenditions on the part of the student interpreter. This could be the result of the nature of the interviews; if the mock interview is intended to challenge the student interpreter, she might face a greater pressure to generate nonrenditions. It is also conceivable that the professional interpreter generates a smaller percentage of nonrenditions in an effort to minimize her influence on the interaction (an ability developed over years of experience as a practitioner). This represents an interesting area for further investigation. It would be useful to conduct a cross-sectional analysis of the percentage (and footing types) of nonrenditions among a group of professional, certified, native signing interpreters. Similarly, it would be useful to conduct a longitudinal study of student interpreters, to determine if and how the percentage of nonrenditions (and their footing types) change over time.

The findings here indicate the benefit of additional research in the area of interpreters' footings. In future research, with a larger corpus of data, it would be beneficial to attempt to identify consistent patterns within which various types of footing occur, and within which interactional outcomes appear to be effectively realized. This will assist in determining how interpreters' choices regarding code and footing type influence interactive discourse. While an interpreter might make conscious choices about the inclusion of certain nonrenditions (such as a summons or an explanation), an interpreter cannot help but make choices about linguistic code when generating utterances. Research regarding the impact of code choices on interactional discourse indicates that code switches can have a profound impact upon the outcome of an encounter (Gumperz 1982). Thus, an interpreter cannot help but make choices that influence the outcome of the interaction, and that, in some way, influence the participants' perceptions of one another. This being the case, a profound question emerges for professional interpreters. Should interpreters, recognizing that they cannot help but function as a participant within an interpreted encounter, no longer strive to be a neutral, uninvolved participant or should they recognize the paradox of neutrality and strive to minimize their influence on interactive discourse?

5

The Interpreter's Paradox

INTERPRETERS, like other participants, bring their own frames and schema to interpreted encounters. Moreover, analysis of interpreter-generated utterances that are not renditions of other-party discourse indicates that interpreters' contributions can be categorized into two types: relayings and interactional management. Regardless of which type of footing an interpreter employs, each utterance requires that a choice be made about the code in which the utterance is conveyed. The fact that three-quarters of the interpreters' nonrenditions are accessible only to the Deaf participants raises questions about interpreter partiality. Examination of interpreters' footing types reveals that interpreter neutrality is a complex notion.

What is interpreter neutrality? If interpreters add no interpreter-generated contributions to the interaction, certain information that is normally accessible in interactive discourse would be missing. If equivalency is supposed to be a marker of neutrality, certainly the omission of this type of information would detract from neutrality. Thus, an interpreter's offering "extra" information or utterances in order to provide equal information actually minimizes the interpreter's influence on the interaction.

Despite suggestions that an interpreter's presence is best left unnoticed (Fink 1982), introducing and identifying participants' roles within interaction is an accepted practice. Providing no introduction of an interpreter can leave participants feeling confused about who to talk to and how the interaction should proceed. Introducing an interpreter provides the opportunity not only to clarify the interpreted encounter frame, but to try to align participants' schema regarding that frame prior to the development of interactional problems. Who should be responsible for such introductions and how they might best be carried out is an area for further investigation.

Interpreters responding to questions or interference have the opportunity to provide no response, minimal conventional responses, or longer explanations. It appears that nonresponses represent marked behavior and actually cause more interactional problems than do responses. Minimal responses appear to fulfill conventional requirements with the least amount of interference to either the interaction itself or the interpreter's ability to provide renditions of it. Further investigation is needed not only with regard to types of responses in various situated encounters, but also regarding which participants receive explanations. If interpreters provide more explanations to Deaf participants than to hearing participants, there is a question as to the impact of this apparent partiality on interpreted interactions.

Interpreters' nonrenditions cannot be assumed a priori to be extraneous information. Some aspects of the discourse are conveyable only through interpreter-generated nonrenditions. Moreover, some interpreter-generated nonrenditions could provide procedural information in an attempt to avoid interactional problems evolving from the interpreter's presence later in the interaction. Thus, certain footing types can be seen as avenues for minimizing the interpreters' influence on the discourse. Moreover, interpreters influence the interactive discourse to different degrees depending, in part, on their marked or unmarked responses. Although the interpreters appeared to attempt to limit their influence through nonresponses (at least to the hearing participants), findings suggest that minimal responses are actually less marked, and therefore less disruptive, than either nonresponses or explanations. Apparently, the concept of "neutral" interpreter behavior is better defined by situated interactional norms and expectations than by predefined constraints resulting in marked interactional behavior.

In order to determine how the interpreters impacted the encounters in which they interpreted, it is possible to examine the ways in which various types of footing within the interpreters' utterances influenced the interaction. Some of the interpreters' footing types created an opportunity for the discourse to proceed in a manner not dissimilar from monolingual interactive discourse. Conversely, other interpreter contributions to the discourse actually misrepresented the footing within the interaction.

Similarities

In monolingual interactive discourse, the fact that participants share both a language and the mode in which it is transmitted means that participants generally have access to not only the content of utterances, but also the fact that an utterance is occurring and from where it originates. Moreover, participants in monolingual interaction most likely either know one another, or have the means to discover the identity and relevance of another participant's presence. That is, people generally introduce themselves (or one another) and include pertinent information regarding relationships to one another and, hence, to the interactive event (e.g., "This is my sister, Wendy"). Thus, introductions of interpreters in interactive events can be seen as similar to introductions of any unknown participant. Once an event has gotten under way, conventions exist for addressing unplanned interruptions within interactions. Interpreters following these conventions exhibit unmarked behavior similar to that encountered in noninterpreted interaction. All of these areas that occur within monolingual interaction also can be found in the interpreted encounters examined here. Discussion of these issues can help to elucidate some of the complexities associated with the notion of interpreter neutrality.

Turn-Initiation and Voice Recognition

In monolingual interactive discourse, when an interlocutor begins an utterance, addressees are generally able to determine that a turn has been initiated and who is the source of that turn, in addition to receiving access to the content of the utterance. How this is accomplished in ASL and English discourse is somewhat different, however. When interpreting between two distinct modalities, information about the occurrence and source of an original utterance might not be accessible to participants without an interpreter-generated contribution. Therefore, for ASL-English interpreters, the rendering of all three parts of an utterance is an important consideration. Because this discourse-relevant information is not directly available to participants who are native to languages conveyed in two different modes, there is the potential for participants to experience confusion regarding who is the original source of a given utterance, or even when another participant begins a turn.

In English monolingual interaction the interlocutors are generally able to hear when someone begins a turn at talk. On the basis of prior exposure to the speaker's voice, the addressee or overhearer can generally identify the speaker (as a familiar person or someone unknown). Similarly, in ASL turns are initiated in part on the basis of eye gaze. When an addressee is not gazing in the direction of an interlocutor who is initiating a turn, the potential addressee is summoned until eye contact is made, allowing the turn to begin.

The interpreters convey this information by generating utterances. These utterances (e.g., a summons or source attribution) provide the information normally accessible in monolingual interaction. Thus, the interpreter-generated contributions can be seen to function in a manner that makes the interpreted interaction similar to monolingual interactive discourse. That is, each participant receives information similar to the information that would be accessible in a monolingual interview. It is important to reiterate that the interpreters did not always provide this information consistently. The issue here is that such contributions seem to represent a similarity to monolingual interaction. Clearly, a difference is that the interpreter has the power to omit information that is, by necessity, always present in monolingual discourse.

Identifying Participant Roles

The only time one of the interpreters provides an identification of her role in the interaction is in the mock encounter. The student interpreter introduces herself as the "sign language interpreter." Although noninterpreted encounters do not have interpreter introductions, they often include introductions of unknown participants. Such introductions often include reference to the participant's role within the encounter (as the doctor or nurse, husband or wife, etc.). Thus, introduction of an interpreter can be seen as similar to noninterpreted encounters, where participant identification is not uncommon. Nevertheless, the way in which an interpreter's role is identified can make a difference in the progression of the interaction.

One issue with regard to identification of the interpreter's role is who controls the introduction. In the mock medical interview, the interpreter introduction is handled by the interpreter herself. In the actual medical interview there is no formal introduction, but when the interpreter's participant status is questioned by the doctor, the Deaf participant explains the interpreter's role. It is conceivable that any of the participants could introduce the interpreter, and each participant introduction would convey a certain participant alignment within the interaction from that point on. For example, when the Deaf mother explains the interpreter's function, the "patient" and the interpreter appear to be aligned and the doctor excluded; he is the one who does not understand. This Deaf participant-interpreter alignment is created despite the fact that the doctor and Deaf participant may have met before, whereas the Deaf participant and the interpreter have not. It is conceivable that the sharing of a common language (ASL) creates a unique bond. It is also likely that where the doctor has never worked with an interpreter before, the Deaf participant has experienced interpreted encounters for many years. Thus, both the Deaf participant and the interpreter share a familiarity with the social roles, if not with one another as individuals. One of the potential problems with an introduction generated by the Deaf participant as a "patient" (or parent of patient) is that it could threaten the doctor's position as the expert and higher-status interlocutor by placing him or her in the less experienced, naive, or student role. Although such a challenge might not be undesirable, it could influence the quality of care received by a Deaf patient.

It is also conceivable that the doctor could introduce the interpreter or explain her function. Frequently, it is the institution that

is responsible for hiring the services of an interpreter, and as professional service providers the doctor and interpreter could share a bond
(in addition to that of a shared language, in this case, English). One
of the potential problems in this case is that the Deaf person is the
minority group member. Since hearing people represent an oppres-
sor group (and most interpreters are hearing), seeing an alignment
between the doctor and the interpreter could be uncomfortable for
the Deaf participant.

A third possibility, and the one seen in the mock interview, is
that the interpreter introduces herself. The issue inherent in this option is that the interpreter must make code choices. When the student interpreter attempted to introduce herself while both speaking
and signing at the same time, her utterances were awkward and in-
accurately produced (at least the signed portion). On the other hand,
if an interpreter chooses to introduce herself in one language at a
time there is still a question of who receives the introduction first.
Once again, the interpreter's choice could reflect some partiality
with regard to one or another participant. Treating either participant
in a partial manner can influence the subsequent interaction and the
quality of medical care. The doctor might feel threatened, and the
patient might feel unwilling to share details of personal history.
Clearly, further investigation regarding the ways in which interpreter introductions are handled and their impact on the medical interview is necessary.

A second issue with regard to the identification of the interpreter's role is related to the interaction of frames and schema. The
student interpreter introduces herself as the sign language interpreter. However, she does not elaborate on the function of an interpreter within an interaction. Thus, while all the participants share
the interpreted encounter frame, there is a mismatch in their
schema for that frame. Because there is a mismatch in the schema
related to the interpreted encounter frame in both cases, it is possible that all the participants in interpreted encounters could benefit
from briefly addressing the interpreter's function. As McIntire and
Sanderson (1995) point out, interpreters do not always function in
a consistent manner. An interpreter might function differently

depending on the situation and the participants. Thus, it is even more critical that all participants share a similar schema for the interpreted encounter frame, as it is situated within a particular interpreted encounter.

Because of the social roles adopted by the Deaf and hearing participants in the two cases under examination here (doctor as hearing, and patient, or parent of patient, as Deaf), this discussion has focused on the implications of introductions based on hearing doctor and Deaf patient roles. In future research it would be interesting to examine this issue in medical interviews in which the doctor is Deaf and the patients are either Deaf or hearing. Nevertheless, for the present discussion it is clear that the inclusion of interpreter introductions in interpreted interaction is similar to the introductions that are frequently a part of interactive, multiparty discourse. Who should be responsible for the introductions, and what information should be included are areas that warrant further research. The results of such research could provide a basis for both professional guidelines and for interpreter education programs.

Following Discourse Conventions

Interpreters, as participants within an interaction, are subject to interference from the physical environment, as are all the participants. In addition, other participants are capable of addressing the interpreter at any time during the interaction. When faced with such circumstances, the interpreters have the option of not responding, responding minimally, or providing lengthy responses and explanation to one or more of the other participants. There are often certain conventions for participant responses. For example, a request for information conventionally receives some sort of response, even if it is an indication that the information is unknown or unavailable. Whether or not interpreters follow these conventions can determine the ways in which the interpreter influences the interactive discourse.

It has become clear that both interpreters avoid responding when addressed by the hearing participants. In both cases, the nonresponses lead to awkward or problematic moments in the discourse. For example, the student interpreter avoids answering the hearing participant's question about how to sign "ulcer." The result is not only confusion, but some of the discourse is not interpreted into ASL (while the interpreter elicits a response from the Deaf participant). In this example, the hearing participant is left with an un-filled slot in a question-answer adjacency pair. Conversely, when the student interpreter provides minimal, noncomplying responses to the Deaf participant's requests, there is no unfilled slot and the discourse proceeds. The interpreter's use of a minimal response is a way of fulfilling the need for a second part in the adjacency pair.

The use of adjacency pairs can also occur as a result of interference. Like Schegloff's (1972) discussion of telephone conversations in which the ring of the phone is the first part of an adjacency pair (the summons), interference in the environment can create first parts that conventionally require a second part. At one point in the mock medical encounter, the interpreter accidentally touches the hearing participant. The interpreter, perhaps recognizing the potential interpretation of the touch as a summons, says, "'Scuse me." It appears that the touch is interpreted as a summons by the hearing participant. She stops speaking, gazes at the interpreter, and asks, "Is there a problem?" These two utterances overlap with one another. The interpreter's apology is brief and indicates that the touch is not a summons, but an accident. The interpreter's minimal response allows the interaction to resume.

It is interesting to note that while the interpreter's response to the hearing participant is minimal in the preceding example, her response to the situation with regard to the Deaf participant is not. She provides an explanation of the brief interaction, during which time she is not interpreting the doctor's continuing discourse. The use of explanations, as in this case, sometimes causes interruptions within the interaction. However, other explanations, such as explanations about the nurse coming to the door as a way of introducing the upcoming speaker, do not seem to interfere with the discourse. In fact, in the latter case, the explanation seems to function as a summons and a source attribution; without them, some of the interactional information normally a part of monolingual interactive discourse would be missing.

The use of various types of responses to interlocutors, or to interference, seems to impact differently on the ways in which the interactive discourse itself is influenced. In the two cases under examination here, the use of minimal responses (as opposed to no
response or lengthy explanations) allows the interaction to resume
with the least amount of influence from the interpreter. It appears
that nonresponses, which do not follow conventions of interactive
discourse, cause more interruptions than responses. The interpreters' use of minimal responses creates a situation most similar to
noninterpreted interactive discourse.

Differences

Interpreter footings, including source attribution, summonses, introductions, interference, and explanations could be perceived as
contributing to the interaction in such a way that the interpreted
discourse is similar to noninterpreted discourse. Nevertheless, these
footings are not always consistently maintained by the interpreters.
For example, source attribution is not included in every interpreter
utterance, despite the fact that each utterance has the potential to
represent utterances by at least two participants (the interpreter or
the "other" language user). Further, while some footing types clearly
have the potential to contribute to discourse so that it is similar to
noninterpreted interaction, these same footings can distinguish the
interaction as an interpreted one. For instance, depending on who
controls an introduction and what information it contains, the presence of an interpreter introduction can create interactional alignments unique to interpreted discourse. In addition to these potential
differences, the two cases under examination exhibited a profound
difference between the interpreted interviews and noninterpreted
interviews in the representation of footing within renditions.

Misrepresentation of Footing

Neither the student interpreter nor the professional interpreter responds directly to the hearing participants. In the actual medical interview, one of the strategies used to avoid responding to questions
directed toward the interpreter is to relay the question. In this case,

the Deaf participant responds to the question and the interaction proceeds. However, upon closer examination of the interpreter's rendition, it becomes clear that she alters the footing from the original utterance. As will be seen shortly, this has an important impact on the interpreted interactive discourse.

In the following example (seen earlier in example 4.24), the doctor directs a question to the interpreter. He is requesting clarification regarding the interpreter's rendition of the mother's utterance that indicates she tried to give her son something after he vomited:

Example 5.1

55

D: You (points to interpreter) tried or she (points to mother) tried?

In the doctor's utterance it is clear that he is addressing the interpreter because of his point to her while he uses the second-person pronoun. Despite the fact that the doctor uses the second-person pronoun to refer to the interpreter, and refers to the mother in the third person, the interpreter's rendition of this utterance does not:

Example 5.2

56

I: (taps mother's knee) PRO.1 TRY OR PRO.2 TRY?

                I tried or you tried?

In this example, the interpreter has altered the footing of the utterance from that in the doctor's original utterance. She might have a reason for doing so. For example, it might be a clearer way of rendering a complicated moment in the discourse. Regardless of the rationale, however, the rendition does contain a misrepresented footing; that is, in this particular utterance, it is not clear to the Deaf participant that the doctor is speaking *about* her rather than to her.

In this instance, the Deaf participant begins an explanation of the interpreter's function. This example represents a point of interactional confusion in the discourse.

The fact that the interpreter relays an utterance with a change in footing at this point in the interaction is not surprising. Confusion about the process of interpreted discourse and the function of the interpreter is evident in this encounter (the doctor is not certain whether the interpreter is also a caretaker of the child). However, if the footing in interpreted discourse is misrepresented in other contexts as well, then the interpreter can be seen to impose a tremendous influence on the interaction. That is, if the Deaf participant does not know that she is being talked *about*, she has no power to request that she be spoken to, or to otherwise address the situation. Schiffrin (1993) discusses various possible reasons for speaking *about* another participant. For example, one might speak about another as a way of showing support for them. Conversely, assumptions of communicative incompetence can accompany such a footing. Given these very different alignments, it is significant that a participant might not have access to the fact that he or she is being talked about. Because this participant-participant footing is misrepresented, it becomes clear that it is worth examining the interpreters' relaying of footing within renditions.

Interpreter Pronoun Use within Renditions

Pronominal reference differs among languages. Therefore, it is important to recognize that the use of a pronoun in an original utterance in one language does not always require the use of a pronoun within the rendition in the other language. For this reason, only the interpreters' explicit use of pronouns is examined. Each pronoun that occurs within a rendition is categorized as either *consistent* with the original, *inconsistent* with the original, or *both*. Consistent pronouns are those that match person[1] (i.e., when a first-person rendition is used to relay a first-person pronoun in the original). *Inconsistent* pronouns refer to interpreter's pronouns that do not match the person of the original utterance (as in example 5.2). When pronouns are categorized as *both*, some vacillation within the rendi-

Table 5.1 Occurrences of Pronominal Reference in Student Interpreter's ASL Renditions in Mock Medical Interview

	N	Consistent (%)	Inconsistent (%)	Both (%)
Number of Occurrences	13	6 (46.1%)	5 (38.5%)	2 (15.4%)

tion, and more than one pronoun occurs. These categories are examined for renditions in ASL and English produced by the student interpreter and by the professional interpreter.

An examination of the student interpreter's use of pronouns within ASL renditions indicates that the rendered footings are not always consistent with the original utterances they are intended to relay (see table 5.1). Within the ASL renditions, the student interpreter produces a total of thirteen pronouns. Of these thirteen, only half are consistent with the original utterance. In example 5.3 below, the student interpreter can be seen to use the first-person singular pronoun in ASL to render the doctor's use of first person in the original utterance:

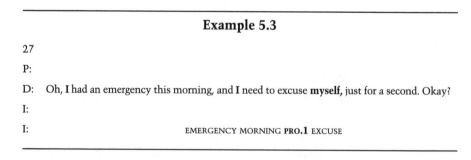

Example 5.3

27

P:

D: Oh, I had an emergency this morning, and I need to excuse **myself,** just for a second. Okay?

I:

I: EMERGENCY MORNING **PRO.1** EXCUSE

It is important to remember that the frequency of pronominal occurrence is not at issue here. Rather, the relevant question is whether or not the interpreter uses a pronoun consistent in person with the pronoun used in the original. In example 5.3 the interpreter clearly does so. Nevertheless, more than half of the ASL pronouns are either inconsistent or contain both consistencies and inconsistencies in the multiple pronoun use. An example of the former can be seen in the following:

Example 5.4

54

P: = AWKWARD PRO.1

D: Well-   y'know it just depends on whether **you** really =

I: = If I don't have it, I'm a wreck.

I:

                                                                   UH =

55

P:

D: = wanna heal or not, uh, r- as I said before, right now this isn't a big problem =

I:

I: = TRUE DEPEND **PRO.1** WANT HEALTH

Example 5.4 begins with the end of the patient's response to the doctor's suggestion that he not drink a lot of coffee. The patient is explaining that he really depends on coffee, or he is a "wreck." The doctor then indicates that whether or not the patient decides to continue to drink coffee is really a matter of his interest in healing. In line 55, the student interpreter can be seen to render the doctor's second-person pronoun (seen in line 54) from the original English utterance as a first-person pronoun in the ASL rendition. This is an example of an inconsistent rendering.

The student interpreter also produces a mixture of both consistent and inconsistent pronouns within her renditions. This can be seen in example 5.5. This example takes place in the beginning of the mock interview, just after the interpreter has introduced herself:

Example 5.5

2

P:

D: Oh, **you're** the interpreter for today.

I: . . . and I'm gonna be the sign langu-language interpreter for today.

I: . . . POSS.1 SIGN LANGUAGE INTERPRETER LANGUAGE NOW. **PRO.1 PRO.2 PRO.1** OH =

3

P: (nods)

D: It's nice to meet you.

I:

I: = INTERPRETER NOW PRO.1 #OH #OK. PRO.1 -   NICE MEET PRO.1

In this example, the interpreter is rendering the doctor's response to her self-introduction. The doctor's use of the second-person pronoun results in a vacillating pronoun use on the part of the interpreter. This vacillation could indicate indecision on the part of the student interpreter as to whether or not she should render the doctor's utterance with the use of constructed dialogue. Indecision is likely the result of limited interpreting experience on the part of the student interpreter. Thus, one possible explanation for the high occurrence of inconsistency and misrepresentation of footings is that the interpreter is an interpreting student. This being a potential cause, it is even more striking to note the contrast in English pronoun use within English renditions (see table 5.2).

The student interpreter produces a total of sixteen English pronouns. All of the pronouns within the English renditions are consistent. An example of this can be seen in 5.6 (p. 171), in which the patient is commenting on his feelings about getting the results of a medical test that he supposedly underwent a week prior to this encounter:

Table 5.2   Occurrences of Pronominal Reference in
Student Interpreter's English Renditions in Mock Medical
Interview

	N	Consistent (%)	Inconsistent (%)	Both (%)
Number of Occurrences	16	16 (100.0%)	0 (0.0%)	0 (0.0%)

Example 5.6

8

Patient:	PRO.1 NERVOUS PRO.1
Doctor:	
Interpreter:	Yeah, **I'm** nervous.
Interpreter:	

The interpreter clearly uses a first-person-singular pronoun in her rendition, just as the patient did in the original utterance. Every instance of pronoun use within the interpreter's English renditions is consistent with the pronoun in the original ASL utterance.

There are several possible explanations for the significant difference between the student interpreter's pronoun use within the ASL and English renditions. One explanation is that the interpreter is better able to provide consistent renditions into her first language. This would support the contention that "simultaneous interpretation can only be done properly into one's native language" (Seleskovitch 1978, 100). A second possibility is that the footing alterations are due to translation issues unique to English-to-ASL renditions. For example, where an English source utterance refers to someone in second or third person, an ASL translation might incorporate constructed dialogue in which the interpreter would take on the "role" of the other and refer to him or her by referring to herself, using a first-person pronoun. A third possibility is that the difference reflects the interpreter's schema regarding interpreted encounters. The student interpreter interacts in different ways with the hearing and Deaf participants. For example, she answers the Deaf participant's questions while refraining from answering questions posed by the hearing participant. It is possible that the interpreter's schema allows her to communicate directly with the Deaf participant but not with the hearing participant. Thus, some of the discourse is relayed as one person telling another what the third person said. Similarly, if the interpreter feels more partial toward the Deaf participant, it is possible that she is more comfortable representing his words as her own, whereas the doctor's words are more comfortably represented as the words of another (e.g., "she said"). Finally, it is possible that the student interpreter is simply demonstrating her current status as an interpreter in training. In order to assess the latter possibility, it is useful to examine the professional interpreter's use of pronouns in renditions.

Examination of the professional interpreter's pronoun use within the ASL renditions reveals that, as in the case of the student interpreter, the rendered footings are not always consistent with the original utterances they represent (see table 5.3). The professional interpreter produces a total of eighty-one ASL pronouns.[2] Unlike the student interpreter, only about one-fourth of the pronouns are inconsistent with the original utterance. An example of an inconsistency was seen earlier in examples 5.1 and 5.2, in which the doctor

Table 5.3 Occurrences of Pronominal Reference in Professional Interpreter's ASL Renditions in Actual Medical Interview

	N	Consistent (%)	Inconsistent (%)	Both (%)
Number of Occurrences	81	61 (75.3%)	18 (22.2%)	2 (2.5%)

clearly addresses the interpreter with a second-person pronoun (pointing to her simultaneously), which she then renders with a first-person pronoun in ASL. The professional interpreter clearly produces fewer inconsistencies within her ASL renditions. Nevertheless, despite the smaller proportion of inconsistency, the fact that one-quarter of the pronouns are inconsistent is significant, especially considering that the professional interpreter grew up with ASL as a native language. Once again, the variation in consistency between the ASL and English renditions is striking.

The professional interpreter produces a total of 115 English pronouns within her renditions. As in the case of the student interpreter, these pronouns are consistent in every case with the original utterances they are intended to relay (see table 5.4). The professional interpreter is a native bilingual, while the student interpreter has learned ASL as a second language. In addition, although the student interpreter is still an interpreter "in-training," the professional interpreter is certified and has years of experience. Thus, on the basis of the two cases under examination here, it appears that the different representations of footings within the ASL and English renditions are not simply due to language background or years of experience. Rather, the difference could be the result of some aspect of the process of rendering messages from English to ASL or could reflect the interpreters' schema in which Deaf participants and hearing participants are treated differently.

Table 5.4 Occurrences of Pronominal Reference in Professional Interpreter's English Renditions in Actual Medical Interview

	N	Consistent (%)	Inconsistent (%)	Both (%)
Number of Occurrences	115	115 (100.0%)	0 (0.0%)	0 (0.0%)

An additional possibility is that the interpreters' pronoun use reflects consistencies and inconsistencies in their input. The Deaf mother in the actual medical interview refers to the hearing doctor and nurse in the second person consistently throughout the interview. This could account for the fact that the professional interpreter consistently refers to the hearing participants in the second person. However, the hearing participants are not consistent in their reference to the Deaf mother. The doctor refers to the mother using second person in less than half of his references to her, using third-person pronominal reference just over half of the time. Similarly, three-fourths of the nurse's pronominal references to the mother are third-person pronouns. Thus, the professional interpreter is faced with recurring shifts in footing in the original English utterances. These shifts could create "leaky" frames for the interpreter. Tannen and Wallat (1987, 1993) describe "leaky" frames in a pediatrician's discourse, when she shifts register among consulting with medical students, with the patient's mother, and with the child patient undergoing examination. While managing these different frames, the doctor occasionally uses a register from her talk with one of the participants in her talk with another, as in using more technical terms while engaged in the "motherese" talk she reserves for the child patient. For the interpreter, "leaky" frames could be the cause of the inconsistencies in her ASL pronoun use.

Unlike the actual medical interview, the Deaf and hearing participants in the mock interview both consistently refer to their interlocutor in second person. Despite this consistency, the student interpreter exhibits inconsistencies in her pronoun use only within the ASL renditions. The fact that the input differs in each case while the output is so similar raises an interesting question for future research: Is this difference the result of language differences or differences in learning on the part of the interpreters. To examine this issue effectively, a larger body of data is necessary.

It has become clear that the interpreters inconsistently relay footings in ASL renditions from a quarter to over half of the time. Whatever the reason that interpreters might alter a footing from the original, the interpreter is (consciously or not) exercising his or her power to withhold information from participants. The misrepresentation of footings within the interactive discourse is inextricably related to the issue of empowerment. For example, if the Deaf participant in the actual medical interview knew she was being talked *about*, she might say something to change that. Without access to the information, she does not have the power to influence the ways in which others align themselves to her through their talk. Whether or not the alteration of footing is inherent in the process of interpreting, it represents a distinct difference between interpreted discourse and noninterpreted discourse.

Implications of Similarities and Differences

Interpreter footings can influence interactive discourse in one of two ways. Some footing types consist of interpreter-generated nonrenditions that actually contribute to the monolingual-interactional quality of the interpreted interactive discourse. Examination of pronoun use in interpreter-generated renditions reveals that the footing within participants' utterances is not always consistently rendered. Discussion of the notion of interpreter neutrality has been based, in part, on the notion of equivalency. As a result, several issues regarding neutrality have been addressed, including strategies for minimizing the differences in interpreted discourse (e.g., by providing information that is normally a part of monolingual discourse), providing minimal responses, and following discourse conventions (e.g., filling second-part slots in adjacency pairs). Clearly, the notion of neutrality in interactive discourse is complex. The primary focus here has been on the interpreters' neutrality with regard to their own utterances. The examination of misrepresented footings indicates that even interpreter renditions are generated by interpreters, though they function to retell utterances originally generated by others. Thus, the interpreters are both participants in the interaction and conveyors of the discourse. How does this paradoxical role manifest itself in terms of the structure of the interactions?

Unique Triadic Structure of the Interpreted Encounters
Interpreters not only generate their own contributions to the discourse, but also generate their renditions of utterances originated by

others. Examination of pronoun use in interpreter renditions reveals that interpreted utterances do not necessarily reflect the original author's footings. This supports the findings of other sociolinguistic research on interpreters, which indicates that interpreters function as participants within the interaction rather than as conduits between other interlocutors. Yet, equally clear is the fact that the interpreters are far more constrained in their participation than are other participants. That is to say, a large proportion of interpreter utterances are retellings or reports of what other participants have said. This unique position within the interaction has raised questions about the nature of three-party interpreted interaction. Interpreted encounters can be seen as dyadic communication between the Deaf and hearing participant, or as a triadic encounter that also includes the interpreter as a participant. In order to better distinguish between these two, it is necessary to examine the issue of interpreters as reporters of other participants' discourse.

Constructed Dialogue

Examination of the interpreters' pronoun use within renditions indicates there is not always consistency in the manner in which renditions are authored by the interpreters. Some of the renditions use pronouns in the target language that match (in person) those in the source utterance, while others do not. Interpreters, as reporters of others' utterances, clearly do not always report exactly what was said. That reported "speech" is not always an exact duplicate of the original utterance is not a new concept to discourse analysts.

Tannen (1989) points out that reported speech is frequently not representative of a "report" at all. Based, in part, on Voloshinov's ([1929] 1986) and Bakhtin's ([1975] 1981) discussions of reported speech as inextricably situated within the context in which the reporting occurs, Tannen suggests that "reported speech" represents creatively constructed discourse of the *reporter* rather than an untainted, neutral report of another's utterance. For this reason, Tannen proposes the term *constructed dialogue,* as opposed to *reported speech.* The notion of constructed dialogue fits well with the findings here regarding interpreters' renditions. The interpreters' "reports" of what others have said frequently represent the *interpreter's footings*, rather than consistently representing the footings of the original utterances.

When interpreters "report" what others have said, they are not reproducing exact duplicates any more than the speakers in the noninterpreted discourse (discussed in Tannen 1989). If the interpreters did attempt to produce exact duplicates, the addressees would not understand them, for they would be repeating a duplicate in the same language as the original. The fact that interpreters are not only "reporting" what another has said, but also doing so in another language, indicates that interpreter renditions are clearly the "words" of the interpreter. This is parallel to the construction of dialogue in noninterpreted discourse, except that for the interpreter the *reported* context and the *reporting* context occur simultaneously. As Hamilton points out (personal communication), the words of others can be reported either directly or indirectly, serving different functions within the discourse. Evidence from the current data suggest that interpreters, like people telling narratives, make such choices for what could be different purposes within the interaction (example 5.5 seems to represent just such a choice on the part of the interpreter). This would be an interesting area for future research.

All of the interpreters' English renditions use pronouns that are consistent in person with the original utterance. When the ASL includes a first-person pronoun, if the English rendition includes a pronoun then it is also first-person. This can be seen in the following example (seen earlier as example 4.17), in which the mother is responding to the doctor's request for her son's shot records:

Example 5.7

138

M: YES (+VOICE) **PRO.1** FUTURE GET #IT =

D:

N:

C:

I: Yeah, =

I:

139

M: = FROM INDEX (right)+ POSS.1 DOCTOR PRO.1 GET CL:G FROM #GT UNIVERSITY =

D:

N:

C:

I: = I will get it- I'll get from my other doctor. I have an appointment - =

I:

140

M: = P-E-D- (to interpreter) #GT UNIVERSITY P-E-D-I-A-T-R-I-C CENTER INDEX (right) =

D: All right

N:

C:

I: = (head tilt left) (head nods) from Georgetown, uh, the pediatric center there?

I:

In this example, the use of first-person pronouns in the original ASL utterances (identifiable in the transcript by the use of PRO.1) are rendered in the first-person by the interpreter in her English constructions of the mother's discourse. It also interesting to note that, in line 139, the interpreter's rendition includes a false start: "I will get it— I'll get it from my other doctor." This false start does not represent a false start in the original utterance. Rather, it reflects the interpreter's false start. Clearly, the interpreter is author of the utterance in the sense that she is originating the words she is uttering in a language and in a manner in which they have never been uttered before. Nevertheless, the content of her utterance is clearly motivated by another's utterance. That is, it is not the interpreter who will be contacting her previous doctor. Thus, while the interpreter is authoring, not merely animating, her renditions, this is still qualitatively different from the authorship of the original utterer. One way to account for this difference would be to examine the conditions for authorship, possibly identifying a continuum of authorship based on a range of features such as ownership of content and form of an utterance. A second possible explanation is that every participant within an encounter is influenced by a range of factors, including their social role and responsibilities and their personal interests in outcomes. Given the latter, the current data indicate that interpreters are not external conveyors of these social and personal aspects of other interactants. Rather, they are themselves participants who bring their own personal interests and social responsibilities to the interaction. For interpreters, attempting to repeat what others utter is a part of their social role.

A second point worth noting is that the interpreter halts her construction of the mother's utterance at the end of line 139. The interpreter is newer to the area than either the mother or the doctor. If the mother and the doctor were communicating in a Deaf participant–hearing participant dyad, they each would have the relevant background knowledge regarding the referent (the pediatric center). However, the interpreter does not share this background knowledge, and she cannot render what she does not understand. This also serves as evidence that the interpreter's renditions are her own.

Tannen's (1989) notion of constructed dialogue has also been applied to ASL discourse (Roy 1989b; Winston 1991, 1992, 1993; Metzger 1995). Yet, even earlier researchers analyzing "reported speech" in ASL describe the use of body shifts, head shifts, eye gaze, and so forth as associated with the representation of another person's utterances in ASL. In this study, attribution of source related to the ASL renditions consists of both body shifts and pointing. These strategies on the part of the interpreter are similar to the strategies used by ASL signers when constructing dialogue in ASL discourse (this has also been referred by numerous terms in the literature, including role shifting, role playing, and identity shifting). In the following excerpt, the interpreter is first constructing the nurse's utterance, and then shifts her body as she constructs the doctor's utterance:

Example 5.8

95

I: #OH D-A-R-N #rr (shifts to side) #HE HAVE FOUR EYE TEETH C-U-T

The interpreter shifts her body position to indicate that she is relaying the words of a different person. This is a common strategy found in ASL constructions of dialogue (Winston 1991, 1992, 1993; Metzger 1995; Liddell and Metzger 1995). While constructed dialogue is often used to represent the real or imagined words of another from a distinct time and place, the interpreter appears to be constructing the dialogue of participants in real time.

Once the interpreters are seen to be constructing dialogue, their role within the interaction becomes somewhat clearer. The interpreter is having a direct conversation with each of the participants, who are unable to have a direct conversation between each other. Thus, three-party interpreted interaction is not a dyadic conversation between the Deaf and hearing participants. Nor is it a triadic conversation between the Deaf participant, the hearing participant, and the interpreter. Instead, the three-party interpreter-interactive discourse is comprised of two overlapping dyads.

Overlapping Dyads

While spoken-spoken or signed-signed language interpreters deal with participants who are presumably not fluent in one another's languages, interpreters who work in signed-spoken language settings encounter a unique phenomenon. That is, the interlocutors not only cannot understand the other language, but even prosodic information, or the fact than an utterance has occurred at all, might be totally unknown to a participant without the interpreter's contributions. Perhaps for this reason, while interpreter–Deaf participant dyads exist and interpreter–hearing participant dyads exist, little or no Deaf participant–hearing participant dyads occur in the data. This contrasts with the assumption that

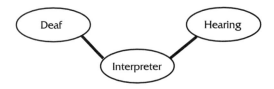

Figure 5.1. Overlapping-dyad view of interpreting.

many people have about the interpreted encounter frame, which relegates the interpreter to a passive, conduit role. Here, the interpreter can be seen to be the pivotal player, the one consistent participant providing the needed overlap between the two separate dyads (see figure 5.1). Contrary to the dyadic and triadic views of interpreting addressed in chapter 1, figure 5.1 represents the overlapping dyadic structure of the two cases of interpreted encounters examined here. Each dyad represents an interaction between two people in one language (interpreter–Deaf participant in ASL; interpreter–hearing participant in English). While it is true that Deaf and hearing participants have opportunities to communicate directly through gestures, paper and pencil, and possibly speechreading, there was little direct communication in this study. On those rare occasions where direct communication was attempted, when the doctor tried to gesture or the mother tapped the doctor's arm, communication was not particularly successful. No significant linguistic dyadic interaction occurred between the hearing and Deaf participants.

As the pivotal point between the two dyads, the interpreter is in a unique position. The interpreter's role within each dyad is essentially to understand what the interlocutor says (which is an interactive task) and to construct information taken from the other dyadic interaction.

The existence of the two overlapping dyads can be seen in the structure of greeting exchanges. In the actual medical encounter, the doctor initiates a greeting when he first enters the examination room:

Example 5.9

40

Mother:		HELLO
Doctor:	(enters) Hello.	
Nurse:		
Child:		
Interpreter:		Hi.
Interpreter:	HELLO	

This example clearly has four parts. When analyzed in the structure of adjacency pairs, a unique form of embedding can be seen (G refers to Greeting, thus G_1 is the first part of the adjacency pair, and G_2 is the second part). As can be seen in figure 5.2, the exchange of greetings reflects the two dyads. When the doctor initiates a greeting exchange in the English dyad (G_1), the interpreter immediately initiates a greeting in the ASL dyad (G_{1a}). When the Deaf participant provides a second part pair (G_{2a}), the interpreter fills the slot within the English dyad (G_2). According to Schiffrin (1987), "An initial greeting constrains the next available interactional slot." Yet, though the initial greeting is followed by a greeting generated by the interpreter, the interpreter's utterance is not seen as a second greeting. Instead, the interpreter's greeting is treated as an initial greeting itself. Thus, in this example, an adjacency pair is initiated by the hearing participant in English, and the ASL adjacency pair, initiated by the interpreter, is embedded within the English exchange. The

G_1 Hearing participant: Hello

G_{1a} Interpreter: HELLO

G_{2a} Deaf participant: HELLO

G_2 Interpreter: Hi

Figure 5.2. Interpreted greeting exchange.

existence of the embedded exchange structure serves as evidence of the overlapping dyadic structure of the interpreted encounters.

The existence of overlapping dyads can also be seen in the following example, in which the doctor attempts to clarify the referent of a pronoun found in the English discourse. This example was seen earlier, and is repeated below for convenience:

Example 5.10

54

M: VOMIT EVERY TIME PRO.1 TRY GIVE PRO.3 (neutral) SOMETHING VOMIT . . . #SO =

D: And the fever's -

N:

C:

I: And he threw up, um, **and every time he threw up I tried to give him something,** so- =

I:

55

M: = PRO.1 GIVE-UP . . .   E-V-E-N L-I-Q-U-I-D-S   PRO.1

D: **You (points to interpreter) tried or she (points to mother) tried?**

N:

C:

I: = I don't know: I- (looks at doctor) I tried =

I: (waves)

56

M: = PRO.1 ++ (glances to interpreter) NO (taps doctor's arm) PRO.3 INTERPRETER-

D:

N:

C:

I: = to give him liquids too.

I: (taps mother's knee) PRO.1 TRY OR PRO.2 TRY?

57

M: = LET PRO.1 EXPLAIN. WHEN INTERPRETER TRUE INTERPRET, PRO.3 WILL =

D:

N:

C:

I: = Now let me explain. When the interpreter is interpreting, she will be speaking =

I:

58

M: = BE TALK A-S I-F PRO.3 NOT I-N ROOM PRO.3. TALK FOR PRO.1, #SO (?off screen) =

D: (chuckles)   Okay, gotcha.

N:

C:

I: = as if, she's not in the room.   She's speaking for me.   So, if it =

I:

59

M: = CONFUSE TRUE TALK PRO.1, A-S I-F PRO.3 PRO.1

D: I'm just interested in the pronoun, that's all.

N:

C:

I: = confuses you, the interpreter's really speaking as if-

I: PRO.1 (REALLY) INTEREST =

60

M: #OK PRO.1

D: You're not taking care =

N:

C: (cries)

I:

I: = WORD "I" (i on chest) PRO.3 (left hand) I (i on chest)

61

M: NO PRO.1 RECENT MEET- (interpreter) #HER FIRST TIME =

D: = of him, you're just interpreting.

N:

C: (crying continues)

I: I just met =

I: NOT PRO.1, PRO.1 NOT TAKE-CARE -

62

M: = NOW.

D: okay   I've been in practice thirty-five years, I've =

N:

C: (screams then crying stops)

I: = her for the first time today, so

I: #OK   PRO. 1 . .   PRO.1 WORK+ + =

This example has provided evidence of mismatches in the participants' schemes regarding interpreted encounters. Evidence of the overlapping dyads can best be seen here by examining the English and ASL portions separately. The ASL portion of the interaction can be seen in example 5.11 below:

Example 5.11

54

M: VOMIT EVERY TIME PRO.1 TRY GIVE PRO.3 (neutral) SOMETHING VOMIT #SO =
     and every time I gave him anything he just threw it up, so =

I:

55

M: = PRO.1 GIVE-UP . . . E-V-E-N L-I-Q-U-I-D-S   **PRO.1**
     I stopped giving him anything, even liquids   ***Me . . .***

I: **(waves)**
                                                        excuse me . . .

56

M: = PRO.1++ (glances to interpreter) NO (taps doctor's arm) PRO.3 interpreter -

      It's me, I did . . .   **No, excuse me, she's the interpreter**

I: **(taps mother's knee)** PRO.1 TRY OR PRO.2 TRY?

                                     Excuse me, I tried (giving him food) or you tried?

57

M: = LET PRO.1 EXPLAIN. WHEN INTERPRETER TRUE INTERPRET, PRO.3 WILL =

           Let me explain. When the interpreter is interpreting, she will =

I:

58

M: = BE TALK A-S I-F PRO.3 NOT I-N ROOM PRO.3. TALK FOR PRO.1, #SO (?off screen) =

           = be talking as if she is not in the room. She's talking for me. So, (?) =

I:

59

M: = CONFUSE TRUE TALK PRO.1, A-S I-F PRO.3 PRO.1

           = confused, she's really talking for me, as if she were me.

I: PRO.1 (REALLY) INTEREST =

                                       I'm really interested =

60

M: #OK PRO.1

                                       okay, I

I: = WORD "I" (i on chest) PRO.3 (left hand) I (i on chest)

           in the word, "I."   *He said, "I."*

61

M: NO PRO.1 RECENT MEET- (interpreter) #HER FIRST TIME =

                    No, I just met her for the first time =

I: NOT **PRO.1, PRO.1** NOT TAKE-CARE -

           It's not me, I'm not taking care of-

62

M: = NOW.

        today.

I: #OK

                   okay.

In the discourse, the first evidence of an interactional problem can be seen in lines 55–56, when the mother produces utterances that do not make sense within the ASL portion of the interaction (translated as follows): "Me . . . it's me, I did . . . No, excuse me, she's the interpreter. . . ." This utterance can be understood by referring back to example 5.6. The doctor has just asked the question designed to clarify who is the caretaker of the child: "You (point to interpreter) tried or she (point to mother) tried?" Apparently, the mother has understood the doctor's confusion here, either as a result of the doctor's visible gestures (pointing), or by speechreading, or both. The mother has understood the doctor despite the fact that the interpreter has not yet rendered it in ASL and is still rendering the mother's prior utterance into English. Though it is rare to see such an occurrence within the data, the fact that the Deaf participant has understood the hearing participant without a rendition seems to argue for the notion of a triadic structure. However, examination of responses to the mother's attempts to respond to the doctor indicates that the link between the mother and the doctor is short-lived.

The interpreter, who is juggling the different frames, does not respond in any way to the mother's utterances in lines 55–56. That is, the interpreter does not respond to the mother, nor does she render the utterances into English for the doctor to hear. Instead, the interpreter completes her renditions of the mother's prior discourse, and attempts to get the mother's attention (by waving at her and tapping her knee in lines 55–56) in order to render the doctor's request for clarification. Once the interpreter successfully elicits the mother's attention and renders the doctor's question, the mother begins to explain the role of the interpreter, and the interpreter renders this into English. Because the mother does not successfully communicate directly with the doctor, even after tapping him on the arm (in line 56), no stable connection between the mother and the doctor can be found within the discourse. The interaction as a whole proceeds smoothly only after the mother and the interpreter resolve their interactional problems.

Further evidence of interactional problems can be seen in the interpreter's pronoun use as shown in lines 59–61. The interpreter, who is rendering into ASL utterances initiated by the doctor, uses the first-person pronoun found in line 59 to refer to the doctor (translated as follows): "I'm really interested in the word 'I.'" In line 60, however, the interpreter shifts footing, and uses a third-person pronoun to refer to the doctor, "He said 'I.'" This utterance is generated by the interpreter, and looks like an attempt to clarify the confusion about who is authoring first-person pronouns. Finally, in line 61, the interpreter renders the doctor's question about whether she (the interpreter) is caretaker of the child, or simply an interpreter. The interpreter uses a first-person pronoun, in this case, to refer to herself, "It's not me, I'm not taking care of—." Whether the mother recognizes the shift as part of a rendition, or perceives the utterances as additional clarification from the interpreter, she clearly understands the point, as is evidenced by her response in line 61. The mother indicates that she has first met the interpreter that very day, and refers to the interpreter with an emphasized English pronoun, finger-spelling H-E-R to assist in alleviating the confusion over pronominal reference.

Part of what characterizes the ASL portion of the interaction is a shifting of footing on the part of the interpreter, sometimes using first person to refer to the doctor and other times to refer to herself. Despite the fact that this shifting could be confusing, the mother exhibits no difficulty in responding appropriately to the questions that are raised. That is, the mother and the interpreter have successfully interacted.

Having examined the ASL portion of the interaction, it is useful to examine the English portion as well. The English interaction, as accessible to the monolingual doctor, is provided as example 5.12.

Example 5.12

54

D: And the fever's -

I: And he threw up, um, and every time he threw up **I tried** to give him something, so . . . =

55

D: **You (points to interpreter) tried or she (points to mother) tried?**

I: = I don't know: I- (looks at doctor) I tried =

56

D:

I: = to give him liquids too.

57

D:

I: = Now let me explain. **When the interpreter is interpreting, she will be speaking =**

58

D: **(chuckles)**   **Okay, gotcha.**

I: **= as if, she's not in the room.**   **She's speaking for me.**   So, if it =

59

D: I'm just interested in the pronoun, that's all.

I: = confuses you, the interpreter's really speaking as if-

60

D: **You're not taking care =**

I:

61

D: **= of him, you're just interpreting.**

I: **I just met =**

62

D: okay

I: **= her for the first time today, so**

In this portion of the interaction, the doctor hears the interpreter say, "I tried to give him something" (line 54). This sounds as if it is the interpreter who is caring for the child, and the doctor asks for clarification, as seen in line 55. Within the English portion of the interaction, a brief pause occurs after his request, at which point the interpreter says, "Now let me explain. When the interpreter is interpreting, she will be speaking as if she's not in the room." The fact that the interpreter uses third person to refer to herself is very odd, and the doctor chuckles at this point in line 58. When the interpreter utters, "She's speaking for me," there is again the opportunity for confusion, since the interpreter is referring to herself in the third person, and to the mother in the first person. Though the doctor indicates that he understands in line 58, "Okay, gotcha," he requests further clarification in lines 60–61 when he asserts, "You're not taking care of him, you're just interpreting." This utterance is clearly directed to the interpreter. From the perspective of the doctor, the interpreter appears to finally respond directly to his request in lines 61–62, when she says, "I just met her for the first time today, so." However, access to the complete interaction (example 5.10) makes clear what the doctor cannot know from the English portion of the interaction alone. The interpreter did not initiate the utterance in lines 61–62. This is merely another rendition of what the mother has originated. The fact is that the interpreter never responds directly to the doctor's request. This information is irrelevant to the progression of the English dyadic encounter.

Through examination of the interaction with regard to the two separate languages, it is clear that a dyadic interaction occurs within each. Yet, these two dyadic interactions are not separate from one another. Evidence of interactional problems exists in both dyadic segments. The interpreter is the link between the two dyads, either in the conveying of information (e.g., to the doctor, that mother and interpreter had first met that very day), or in the relaying of information (e.g., when the mother's explanation is not relayed). Clearly, these examples demonstrate that two separate dyads, one in each language, are connected via the interpreter. The interpreter functions as the pivotal point between the two, either by providing access to the content of one dyad to the addressee in the other, or through failure to do so (as in the mother's unrendered utterances). In fact, confusion over the referents of first-person pronouns is in itself evidence that the interpreter serves as the pivotal link. The doctor recognizes a question about to whom the first-person-singular pronoun refers, and addresses his dyadic partner (the interpreter) in an attempt to discover the answer.

In order to test the existence of overlapping dyads it is also useful to examine a segment of the interaction in which no interactional problems are apparent. The following three examples occur just before the physical examination of the child begins. The doctor and the mother are discussing the nature of the child's visit to the same doctor's office the prior week. Example 5.13 represents the ASL portion of the interaction:

Example 5.13

78

M:

I: PRO.3 (baby) HERE BEFORE PRO.3
                                                            He was here before.

79

M: # WAS HERE LAST-WEEK THURSDAY-   FRIDAY, PRO.1 FORGET PRO.3 NOT =
     He was here last Thursday or Friday, I can't remember which day.   He doesn't =

I:

80

M: = SEEM IMPROVE BETTER HAVE F-E-V-E-R (palm up)
     = seem to have gotten better, he still has a fever . . .

I: #WELL TRUE =
                                                            Well, that =

81

M:

I: = DIFFERENT THING BEFORE. PRO.3 HAVE FAT-NOSE NOSE RIGHT? =
   was for a different thing. He had a stuffed nose, right!

82

M: NO NOT- NOW- NO BEFORE LAST-WEEK HAVE F-E-V-E-R PRO.1 =
   No not- today- No, last week he had a fever =

I: = S-T-U-F-F-Y NOSE. NOW TALK ABOUT F-E-V-E-R =
  = a stuffy nose. Now you're talking about a fever.

83

M: = BRING I-N BETTER F-E-V-E-R STILL OBSERVE SAY THAT PRO.3 SEEM FINE =
  = I brought him in and his fever had improved but they examined him and said he was fine =

I:

84

M: = NONE SEEM WRONG AND THAT TRUE SEEM (blocked by nurse) BECAUSE =
  = that nothing seemed to wrong, and that he really seemed (?) because =

I:

85

M: = TEETH (palm up)
  = of his teething, so . . .

I: #OK
             okay

Within the ASL discourse in the preceding example, the interaction proceeds smoothly. No questions regarding referents occur in
the discourse. Though there is disagreement, responses are appropriate to the questions that precede them. Thus, this segment of the
interaction serves as evidence of the existence of the ASL dyad. Evidence of the existence of the English dyad can be seen in example
5.14. This example represents the English portion of the same segment of the interview:

Example 5.14

78
D: He's been here before by the way, uh Doctor um, =
I:

79
D: = (?) saw him, uh
I: Yeah, he was here last week on Thursday, er- it was Thursday or Friday, =

80
D: Well, it was a total =
I: = I'm not sure but, it doesn't seem like he's gotten any better.

81
M:
D: = different kind of a thing the last time. He had a stuffy nose? he had, y'know, he had-now =
I:

82
D: = we're talkin' about fever and vomiting. Last time we were talkin' about cold symptoms.
I: No, last week, he had fever too, =

83
D: Okay, I see
I: = I brought him in and his fever had gotten better but then . . . they- and the doctor said =

84
D:
I: = that it seemed like he was fine, and it seemed like he was unhappy =

85
D: Okay.
I: = because he was teething. (shrugs to doctor)

As in example 5.13, the English discourse in example 5.14 proceeds smoothly and without apparent interactional problems. This segment of the English discourse functions in a manner similar to dyadic, noninterpreted interaction. In the previous two examples, both the ASL and the English dyadic interactions function clearly as if they were whole and complete. In example 5.15 below, both portions will be shown as they occur in the data:

Example 5.15

78

M:

D: He's been here before by the way, uh, Doctor um, =

N: = let me just get one out of two.

C:

I:

I: PRO.3 (baby) HERE BEFORE PRO.3

79

M: #WAS HERE LAST-WEEK THURSDAY-   FRIDAY, PRO.1 FORGET PRO. 3 NOT =

D: = (?) saw him, uh

N:

C:

I: Yeah, he was here last week on Thursday, er- it was Thursday or Friday, =

I:

80

M: = SEEM IMPROVE BETTER HAVE F-E-V-E-R (palm up)

D: Well, it was a total =

N:

C:

I: = I'm not sure but, it doesn't seem like he's gotten any better.

I: #WELL TRUE=

81

M:

D: = different kind of a thing the last time. He had a stuffy nose? he had, y'know, he had-now =

N:

C:

I:

I: = DIFFERENT THING BEFORE. PRO.3 HAVE FAT-NOSE NOSE RIGHT? =

82

M: NO   NOT-   NOW-   NO BEFORE LAST-WEEK HAVE F-E-V-E-R PRO.1 =

D: = we're talkin' about fever and vomiting. Last time we were talkin' about cold symptoms.

N:

C:

I: No, last week, he had fever too, =

I: = S-T-U-F-F-Y NOSE. NOW TALK ABOUT F-E-V-E-R

83

M: = BRING I-N BETTER F-E-V-E-R STILL OBSERVE SAY THAT PRO.3 SEEM FINE =

D: Okay, I see

N:

C: (crying)

I: = I brought him in and his fever had gotten better but then . . . they- and the doctor said =

I:

84

M: = NONE SEEM WRONG AND THAT TRUE SEEM (blocked by nurse) BECAUSE =

D:

N: (enters)

C: (wails)

I: = that it seemed like he was fine, and it seemed like he was unhappy =

I:

85

M: = TEETH (palm up)

D: Okay.   Ask her to just =

N:

C:

I: = because he was teething (shrugs to doctor)

I: #OK

The two dyads overlap within the same stretch of discourse, pivoting around the single participant who is engaged in both dyads: the interpreter. The overlap is best described in terms of the exchange structure (see figure 5.3).

In line 78, the doctor initiates an exchange with his assertion about a prior visit (A_1). The interpreter then initiates an embedded assertion (A_{1a}), which receives a confirmation from the mother as response (R_{2a}). The response within the original exchange is then rendered by the interpreter (R_2). As can be seen in example 5.11, the exchanges overlap in time with one another. That is, A_{1a} begins before A_1 is completed. Similarly, R_2 begins before R_{2a} is completed. The interpreter, as the only participant whose utterances appear in both the original and the embedded exchanges, is the link between the two overlapping dyads within the interpreted discourse.

Despite views of interpreted interaction in which the interpreter is seen as a passive conduit or bridge conveying messages between a Deaf-hearing dyad, or in which the interpreter is seen as a participant in a three-party interaction, the findings here indicate that both the interpreted mock and actual medical interviews actually consist of two overlapping dyads. The use of constructed dia-

A_1 Doctor: He's been here before by the way, uh Doctor um, (?) saw him, uh

    A_{1a} Interpreter: PRO:3 (baby) HERE BEFORE PRO:3

    R_{2a} Mother: #WAS HERE LAST-WEEK THURSDAY- FRIDAY, PRO:1 FORGET

R_2 Interpreter: Yeah, he was here last week on Thursday, er- it was Thursday or Friday

Figure 5.3. Interpreted Exchange

logue by the interpreters and the structure of the greeting exchange in the actual medical interview provide linguistic evidence in support of the overlapping-dyad view of interpreting. This analysis indicates that the situated utterances by participants within the interaction and the sequential structure of the interaction as a whole is not the same for the interpreted interviews as it would be in noninterpreted discourse. While an interpreter can pursue strategies to minimize the intrusiveness of this difference (e.g., through filling second-pair slots with minimal responses), the fact remains that interpreters do influence interactive discourse. Thus, as Baker-Shenk (1991) suggests, interpreters ought to be making intentional choices about those influences.

Implications

It has been seen here that both the student and professional interpreters do influence the medical interview discourse. Further investigation with a larger body of data is warranted in order to seek broad patterns within interpreted medical interviews, other genres of discourse, and across language types (that is, interpreted encounters other than ASL-English). Nevertheless, the analysis here has implications regarding interpreter practice, interpreter education, and, of course, linguistics.

ASL-English Interpreters in Medical Settings

In practice, ASL-English interpreters in medical settings should be alert to the fact that each participant brings a unique schema to the interpreted encounter. As a result, medical interpreters should be prepared to follow two important steps to assist in reducing the impact of mismatches in schema. First, it would be useful for interpreters to monitor research regarding the most effective strategies for achieving the goals of interpreted encounters. As McIntire and Sanderson (1995) indicate, ASL-English interpreters currently apply different models of interpreting at different times. Moreover, Wadensjö (1992) suggests that interpreters often must improvise strategies for coping with the unpredictable circumstances that arise in actual interpreted encounters. However, systematic research regarding the nature of interpreters' strategies and the impact of various strategies in a variety of settings could assist in identifying whether or not certain models of interpreting are best applied or avoided in a given setting, and what types of interpreter strategies are likely to yield desired outcomes.

Medical interpreters who participate in or keep abreast of such research will be best prepared to do the job and to perform the second step, which involves interpreters' providing information to Deaf and hearing consumers about interpreted interviews so that all participants can begin to share similar schema regarding the interpreted encounter frame. Because of the difficulties inherent in providing such information at the time of an interview, it would be useful to develop more global strategies for informing Deaf and hearing consumers.[3] This information sharing should be available not only to medical practitioners and patients, but also to the relatives of patients. Most directly related to the findings here, interpreters should be aware of the potential impact of the presence or absence of interpreter introductions as well as of who provides such introductions and what kind of information is included.

In addition to these two steps, interpreters should be aware of the potential impact of their choices with regard to footing types. Interpreters in medical settings should be aware that code choice can create an appearance of partiality. Patients who feel excluded might not provide as much information as needed to elicit appropriate medical care. Similarly, the services provided by doctors who feel excluded might be influenced. Further research will assist interpreters in this area. Interpreters should also consider the potential impact of added footing types, the omission of discourse-relevant information, and the impact of following certain discourse conventions. For example, it could be useful for interpreters to be aware of the potential impact of nonresponses, minimal responses, or lengthy responses. In this study, some response types create awkward, somewhat tangential exchanges. Given findings regarding doctor-patient communication problems resulting, in part, from doctors' hectic schedules, it seems especially important that interpreters find response-strategies that do not create a need for time-consuming repairs.

Finally, recognition of interpreted encounters as overlapping dyads can help to clarify the two footing types addressed in this study: relayings and interactional management. For example, recognition of the multiple tasks falling on the interpreter as the pivotal point between the two dyads indicates potential benefits for consecutive, rather than simultaneous, interpretation. Consecutive interpretation would allow the interpreter to focus on one dyad at a time, and thus reduce the occurrence of interactional problems. Although it might intuitively seem that there is more time involved in the process of consecutive interpreting, the potential reduction in interactional confusion or misrepresented footings could make consecutive interpretation more time-efficient than simultaneously interpreted interactive discourse. Further investigation of the differences between the two could assist in identifying whether or not certain settings significantly benefit from one or the other.

This study indicates that interpreters influence interactive discourse. The reality of the interpreters' influences is at odds with professionally defined goals (e.g., in professional codes). Interpreters working in medical settings should be aware of this discrepancy. While this study indicates that interpreters' goals are at odds with the reality of interactive discourse, it is beyond the scope of this study to identify a tangible, prescribed solution to this dilemma. What can be seen from this study is that some interpreter-generated contributions are an essential part of the interpretation of interactional equivalence. For example, summoning a participant so they know they are being addressed, and attributing the source of an utterance (information that two monolinguals would know), are essential components of the interaction. A patient might respond differently to medical advice depending on whether it comes from a doctor or from a nurse. These contributions from an interpreter should be a part of the interpretation process, perhaps even more than that seen in the cases examined here. Clearly, it is critical to continue empirically based analyses of naturally occurring interpreted encounters in order to investigate the impacts of this divergence between the ideal and reality. Research should also be gathered to identify the various schema that interpreters and consumers bring to interpreted interaction. If professional interpreters, consumers of their services, and researchers work together, they can identify realistic goals for interpreted interaction and determine which interpreter strategies support those goals.

ASL-English Interpreter Education

Investigation of the frames and schema within interpreted medical interviews requires a larger body of data. Such research should include an examination of many student interpreters from a variety of interpreter education programs. Nevertheless, this comparison of the student interpreter case with the case of the professional interpreter does have some implications with regard to interpreter education. These implications relate to how student interpreters are trained to make choices associated with code and footing, as well as to the use of role plays as a training tool.

On the basis of code choices made by the two interpreters, code choice is an issue that should be addressed in interpreter education. Despite the fact that some have recommended simultaneous code production as a way for interpreters to communicate with Deaf and hearing participants simultaneously to avoid leaving anyone out (Earwood 1983), in the findings here the simultaneously produced utterances are faulty when produced by the student interpreter and nonexistent on the part of the native bilingual professional interpreter. More research with a larger body of data could address this issue. Nevertheless, the findings here support recent research that indicates that simultaneously produced utterances are problematic. Further investigation is needed to determine whether a high proportion of single code utterances (in this case, signed utterances), creates a feeling of exclusion among unratified participants.

Interpreter education programs could also discuss the implications of certain footing types. Introductions are an area that can be problematic and that require further investigation, so this is one area worth addressing in interpreter education. In addition, the student interpreter in the mock interview case occasionally did not follow certain discourse conventions in one or the other of the dyads. For example, she left an unfilled slot in question-answer pairs and provided lengthy nonresponses (e.g., explanations), which created interactional problems. According to this study, the use of minimal responses seemed to be the least problematic in the flow of the discourse. This is an area worth addressing with interpreting students as well.

An additional area found to be lacking in the student interpretation in this study is the summoning of participants. This could be the result of the artificial nature of the role play. Nevertheless, students of ASL-English interpretation should have the opportunity to practice this particular type of footing. One way of gaining such practice and reducing the artificial nature of medical interview role plays is to work with medical students. Although the mock medical encounter has much in common with the actual medical encounter in terms of the interaction of frames and schema and the two categories of interpreter-generated footings, there are also some differences that result, in part, from the fact that a technical redoing is not the same as an actual encounter. For this reason, and in an effort to prepare medical practitioners to work in interpreted encounters, it might be useful for interpreter education programs to team up with medical education programs. The students in both programs could assist one another in learning about the realities of interpreted medical interviews.

The examination of both a student interpreter and a professional interpreter has provided some information relevant to educating interpreters to work in medical settings. Nevertheless, it should not be overlooked that this is a case study. More research is needed to provide detailed information for interpreter educators. Both cross-sectional and longitudinal studies of interpreting students are needed. Such studies should include these interpreters working in classrooms, role plays, and any other settings in which they work. A systematic investigation of student interpreters in such settings can help to determine the effectiveness of such training strategies as role plays. In addition, such research could help to determine the relevance of temporal, sociolinguistic and other factors that impact on interpreter education.

Linguistics

As an applied sociolinguistic examination of interpreted interaction, this study ultimately contributes to the broader field of linguistics. The examination of interactive discourse in any setting provides useful information to those interested in understanding language. For example, while non-data-based or empirically based experimental studies of interpreting comprise the bulk of research on interpreted discourse, the information obtained from this study regarding the interaction of frames and schema, the types and functions of footing produced in interpreter-generated utterances, and the overlapping dyadic structure of the discourse have become clear as a result of the interactional approach and the use of naturally occurring data. The application of sociolinguistics to studies in other areas, such as the study of language changes resulting from such disorders as Alzheimer's or aphasia (Hamilton 1994; Goodwin 1995), provides useful insights regarding language unavailable from noninteractional studies. Similarly, this study provides some information about language not available from noninteractional studies of interpreting. This information includes nonlinguists' assumptions about language as well as information regarding frame theory and potential sequential structures of discourse that could apply in noninterpreted discourse.

According to Shuy (1995), "Tacit theories of language use could not be discovered outside of an interactive context." The examination of interactive discourse can offer insights into such tacit theories held by participants within the interaction. The fact that interpreters generate nonrenditions in order to provide information regarding the fact that an utterance has been initiated and who is the source of the utterance reflects the interpreters' tacit understanding that an utterance contains three parts: its existence, its source, and its content. The fact that this study focuses on interpreted discourse, and that the languages involved occur in two distinct modes (one visual, one acoustic), make the discovery of this tacit assumption about language possible.

This study also proposes a definition of the often conflicting terms applied within frame theory. The definition proposed here is based on the constructs that recur within the literature on frames, schema, and scripts. Building on the linguistic applications of frame theory within single language discourse such as English and ASL, this study expands the application to not only a multicultural context (Watanabe 1993), but to a multilingual one as well.

Examination of the footing functions and types within the interpreted encounters provides support for footing discovered in other settings, and for new types that might yet be found in different contexts. For example, the interpreters' use of constructed dialogue provides a rare opportunity for future investigation of this phenomenon. As Voloshinov ([1929] 1986) indicates, in order to truly understand constructed dialogue it is necessary to examine the relationship between the constructed dialogue and the original utterances upon which it is based. Since interpreters in this study have been found to construct the dialogue of participants in real time, both parts are available for examination. This is an area of linguistic research worth further examination, in both simultaneous and consecutive interpreting contexts.

Finally, another implication for linguistics relates to the sequential structure of the discourse itself. The interpreted encounters can be seen to consist of two overlapping dyads, on the basis of the embedded adjacency pairs. While insertion sequences within adjacency pairs have been addressed in noninterpreted interaction (Schegloff 1972; Merritt 1976), these embeddings are generally accessible to and between the interlocutors. However, the embedded greetings discussed in this study indicate two separate interactions that overlap. This is a unique structure that influences the sequence of the discourse in both the ASL and English dyadic discourse. The implication here is that some types of noninterpreted interaction might include similar embeddings. Schiffrin (1993) and Aronsson (1991) both address the issue of speaking for another (e.g., speaking for a friend or a child). In addition, Rosenfeld (1996) finds an overlapping dyadic structure in her examination of therapeutic discourse. Future research could help to determine whether similar embedded structures occur in other types of discourse.

Conclusion

Examination of the questions raised in chapter 1 of this study has demonstrated that interpreters do influence interactive discourse. The ways in which interpreters and other participants frame the interpreted encounters were presented in chapter 3. The types and functions of interpreter contributions to the discourse were addressed in chapter 4. Thus, the initial question regarding the linguistic differences between a monolingual face-to-face conversation and an interpreted conversation has become clear. In interpreted discourse, the interpreter has the power to influence the interaction not only through interpreter-generated utterances that are not renditions or constructions of others' discourse, but also through a misrepresentation of the source message footings within renditions.

While this study has revealed that interpreters have the power to influence discourse, it has only begun to examine the interpreter's ability to *not* influence interactive discourse. That is, the findings here indicate that some interpreter strategies result in less marked influences within the interaction. Given the professional goal of not influencing discourse, more research regarding an interpreter's ability to limit or constrain their influences in interpreted encounters is needed. In the meantime, this study supports previous sociolinguistic research that shows that interpreters are participants within interactive discourse and not merely conduits to it. Thus, the question for the field of interpreting becomes clear: should interpreters pursue full participation rights within interpreted encounters? Or should interpreters attempt to minimize, where possible, their influence within interpreted interactions? Herein lies the paradox of neutrality.

Notes

1. Neutrality in Translation and Interpretation

1. Signed English codes, often referred to as manually coded English (MCE), are contrived systems that manipulate signs in an attempt to represent the morphology and syntax of English visually. Although there have been problems with the use of MCE as a model for language acquisition (Supalla 1986, 1991), the use of such systems frequently occurs among bilingual adults. While it is possible that bilingual adults are able to make up for any deficiencies in the contrived code as a result of their prior knowledge of both ASL and English, it is also possible that these systems are actually "altered" and might frequently represent a form of contact between English and ASL (Lucas and Valli 1989, 1991, 1992).

2. Analyzing Interpreted Medical Interviews

1. As Roy (1986) points out, the definition of "native speaker" is not as simple in signed language research as it is in spoken language studies. Because the majority of deaf children are born to hearing parents who are not fluent in a signed language, language acquisition issues are often unique for deaf children. As Winston (1993) indicates, many deaf children are not exposed to an accessible, natural language until they attend a residential school at which some students and staff are fluent signers. Thus, the definition of "native" could be based on one or more of a variety of factors (e.g., only those whose parents are fluent signers or also those who are exposed to the signed language at a residential school by a certain age). Roy (1986) finds that the definition used among researchers depends somewhat on the purpose of the research. For this study, the term "native signer" refers to those who either have Deaf parents who sign ASL as a first language, or who were exposed to ASL at a residential school from an early age and who are judged by other native signers to be native users of ASL.

4. Participation Frameworks

1. Whereas spoken language interpreters are not expected to speak two languages simultaneously, ASL-English interpreters might attempt to, or be ex-

pected to attempt to, communicate in both languages simultaneously. Unique features of language contact between signed and spoken languages are addressed by Lucas and Valli 1992.

2. Although not included as a part of the two cases under examination here, the mock medical interview was reenacted by the class with the same student interpreter interpreting. Although there was no discussion of footing shifts per se, it is interesting to note the manner in which the participants decided to improve upon the original mock interview. The awkwardness described with regard to the interpreter's linguistic errors resulting from simultaneous output did not occur in the reenactment.

3. Tannen (1986, 1989) argues that reported speech is not really a report of other people's words. Instead, she suggests that speakers construct the dialogue of other people, altering the original in order to fit the dialogue into the speaker's current context. The use of body shifting (as well as other nonmanual signals) to construct the actions and dialogue of characters in ASL discourse has been discussed by numerous researchers. Previously termed *role shifting* or *role playing*, the first reference to the construction of dialogue and actions in ASL on the basis of Tannen's distinction can be found in Roy (1989b), Winston (1991, 1992, 1993), Metzger (1995), and Liddell and Metzger (1995).

5. The Interpreter's Paradox

1. Pronouns in ASL and English will not match in terms of gender and number. In fact, the issue of person reference in ASL has been questioned. For example, Meier (1991) has suggested that ASL has only a first-person/non-first-person distinction. Regardless of whether or not *person* is distinguished by separate pronominal forms, the *referent* is retrievable from the discourse. Therefore, for the purpose of the current analysis, the relative consistency between pronominal forms will be based on the latter.

2. The total number of ASL pronouns is actually based on the total number visible on the videotape. There are several occasions during which the interpreter's signing is not clearly visible, either because she is off-camera or blocked from the camera's view by one of the other participants.

3. Dissemination of information regarding interpreting services is clearly an area that needs to be pursued. Nevertheless, it is important to mention here that a tremendous amount of research remains to be done. Moreover, many medical practitioners and medical institutions are not even aware of the need to provide interpreters, not only in pursuit of effective communication but also on legal grounds as specified in legislation such as the federal Americans with Disabilities Act. Further, many medical practitioners and medical institutions do not know how to secure professional interpreting services. Clearly, much work remains to be done in this area.

Appendix 1

Registry of Interpreters
for the Deaf
Code of Ethics

©1995 RID, Inc.

Interpreter/Transliterator shall keep all assignment-related information strictly confidential.

Guidelines:

Interpreter/transliterators shall not reveal information about any assignment, including the fact that the service is being performed.

Even seemingly unimportant information could be damaging in the wrong hands. Therefore, to avoid this possibility, interpreter/transliterators must not say anything about any assignment. In cases where meetings or information becomes a matter of public record, the interpreter/transliterator shall use discretion in discussing such meetings or information.

If a problem arises between the interpreter/transliterator and either person involved in an assignment, the interpreter/transliterator should first discuss it with the person involved. If no solution can be reached then both should agree on a third person who could advise them.

When training new trainees by the method of sharing actual experiences, the trainers shall not reveal any of the following information:

Name, sex, age, etc., of the consumer;

Day of the week, time of the day, time of the year the situation took place;

Location, including city, state, or agency;

Other people involved;

Unnecessary specifics about the situation.

It only takes a minimum amount of information to identify the parties involved.

Interpreter/Transliterators shall render the message faithfully, always conveying the content and spirit of the speaker, using language most readily understood by the person(s) whom they serve.

Guidelines:

Interpreter/transliterators are not editors and must transmit everything that is said in exactly the same way it was intended. This is especially difficult when the interpreter disagrees with what is being said or feels uncomfortable when profanity is being used. Interpreter/transliterators must remember that they are not at all responsible for what is said, only for conveying it accurately. If the interpreter/transliterator's own feelings interfere with rendering the message accurately, he/she shall withdraw from the situation.

While working from Spoken English to Sign or Non-audible Spoken English, the interpreter/transliterator should communicate in the manner most easily understood or preferred by the deaf or hard of hearing person(s), be it American Sign Language, Manually Coded English, fingerspelling, paraphrasing in Non-audible Spoken English, gesturing, drawing, or writing, etc. It is important for the interpreter/transliterator and deaf or hard of hearing person(s) to spend some time adjusting to each other's way of communicating prior to the actual assignment. When working from Sign or Non-audible Spoken English, the interpreter/transliterator shall speak the language used by the hearing person in spoken form, be it English, Spanish, French, etc.

Interpreter/Transliterators shall not counsel, advise, or interject
personal opinions.

Guidelines:

Just as interpreter/transliterators may not omit anything which is
said, they may not add anything to the situation, even when they are
asked to do so by other parties involved.

An interpreter/transliterator is only present in a given situation because two or more people have difficulty communicating, and, thus, the
interpreter/transliterator's only function is to facilitate communication. He/she shall not become personally involved because in so doing
he/she accepts some responsibility for the outcome, which does not
rightly belong to the interpreter/transliterator.

Interpreter/Transliterators shall accept assignments using discretion with
regard to skill, setting, and the consumers involved.

Guidelines:

Interpreter/transliterators shall only accept assignments for which
they are qualified. However, when an interpreter/transliterator shortage
exists and the only available interpreter/transliterator does not possess
the necessary skill for a particular assignment, this situation should be
explained to the consumer. If the consumers agree that services are
needed regardless of skill level, then the available interpreter/transliter-
ator will have to use his/her best judgment about accepting or rejecting
the assignment.

Certain situations may prove uncomfortable for some interpreter/
transliterators and consumers. Religious, political, racial, or sexual difference, etc., can adversely affect the facilitating task. Therefore, an in-
terpreter/transliterator shall not accept assignments which he/she
knows will involve such situations.

Interpreter/transliterators shall generally refrain from providing
services in situations where family members, or close personal or professional relationships may affect impartiality, since it is difficult to
mask inner feelings. Under these circumstances, especially in legal settings, the ability to prove oneself unbiased when challenged is lessened.
In emergency situations, it is realized that the interpreter/transliterator
may have to provide services for family members, friends, or close busi-

ness associates. However, all parties should be informed that the interpreter/transliterator may not become personally involved in the proceedings.

Interpreters/Transliterators shall request compensation for services
in a professional and judicious manner.

Guidelines:

Interpreter/transliterators shall be knowledgeable about fees which are appropriate to the profession, and be informed about the current suggested fee schedule of the national organization. A sliding scale of hourly and daily rates has been established for interpreter/transliterators in many areas. To determine the appropriate fee, interpreter/transliterators should know their own level of skill, level of certification, length of experience, nature of the assignment, and the local cost of living index.

There are circumstances when it is appropriate for interpreter/transliterators to provide services without charge. This should be done with discretion, talking care to preserve the self-respect of the consumer. Consumers should not feel that they are recipients of charity. When providing gratis services, care should be taken so that the livelihood of other interpreter/transliterators will be protected. A freelance interpreter/transliterator may depend on this work for a living and, therefore, must charge for services rendered, while persons with other full-time work may perform the service as a favor without feeling a loss of income.

Interpreter/Transliterators shall function in a manner
appropriate to the situation.

Guidelines:

Interpreter/transliterators shall conduct themselves in such a manner that brings respect to themselves, the consumers and the national organization. The term "appropriate manner" refers to:

a) dressing in a manner that is appropriate for skin tone and is not distracting;

b) conducting oneself in all phases of an assignment in a manner befitting a professional

Interpreter/Transliterators shall strive to further knowledge and skills through participation in workshops, professional meetings, interaction with professional colleagues and reading of current literature in the field.

Interpreter/Transliterators, by virtue of membership or certification by the R.I.D., Inc., shall strive to maintain high professional standards in compliance with the code of ethics.

Appendix 2

Transcription
Conventions

ALL SMALL CAPS	Used for English glosses of signs
F-I-N-G-E-R-S-P-E-L-L-I-N-G	Fingerspelling
#LETTERS	The gloss that follows is lexicalized spelling
HYPHENATED-WORDS	Represent a single sign
++	Reduplication of a sign
PRO.1	PRO = Pronoun, 1 = first person, 2 = second person, 3 = third person
POSS.1	Possessive pronoun (and person)
CL	Classifier predicate
Bob-ASK-TO-Mary	Indicating verbs include the subject/object referents
(actions)	Indicate visual/spatial information and some contextual information
...	Pause of half-second or more
-	Interrupted utterance
(?)	Unclear from the video recording
.	Sentence final prosody
,	Clause final intonation
?	Rising intonation (English) or non-manual signals indicating a question form

=   Utterances continuing to the follow-
                                     ing or from the preceding line
Italics   Translation of text on preceding line

The Musical-Score Transcript

The use of a musical-score transcript allows the interpretation to co-
incide with the interpreted utterances as they do in the data. The interpreter has two lines for utterances—one for English, the other for
ASL. Overlapping utterances within a single "line" indicate overlaps. Occasionally, lines will be taken out of this format and addressed in isolation. The use of caps or lowercase indicates a distinction between ASL and English discourse.

Appendix 3

Full Transcript
of Example 3.8

28
P: WAVE PRO.1 DO-DO PRO.1? PRO.3 SAY U-L-C-E-R. PRO.1 (head shake) BELIEVE PRO.3, PRO.1.
    Hey, what do you think I should do? She says I have an ulcer but . . . I don't believe her.
I:

29
P: INVENT PRO.3.
    She's just making it up.
I: PRO.1 MUST ASK-ASK-ASK PRO.1 KNOW-NOTHING U-L-C-E-R
    I think you'd better talk to her. I really don't know anything about ulcers.

30
P: INVENT PRO.3 =
                                                                She's just making it =

I:

31
P: = INVENT. PRO.1 (head shake) TRUST PRO.1 . . . UH U-L-C-E-R TRUE MEANING RIGHT PRO.3?
    = up. I don't trust her . . . hmm, is an ulcer really what she said it is?
I: (nods)

32
P: ASK-ASK? =
                                                          Ask the doctor? =

I: PRO.1 TRUE EXACT KNOW ULCER? NO. PRO.1 ASK-ASK POSS.3.
    I just don't know much about ulcers, it's better to ask the doctor.

33

P: = PRO.1 ASK-ASK CAN'T PRO.1. TRUST PRO.1, CHOKE. DOCTOR PRO.1 UNCOMFORTABLE =
    I can't ask the doctor! I don't trust her. Ugh, doctors . . . it's so awkward

I:

34

P: = PRO.1 ASK-ASK CAN'T. PRO.2 CAN ASK-TO (doctor) PRO.2 CAN . . . ASK-TO (doctor)? UH-
    no way, I can't ask her. Could you ask her? Could you? Uhm-

I:

35

P:

I: PRO.1 HAPPY INTERPRET FOR PRO.2 EVERY-THING . . . ASK-ASK (doctor reenters)
    I'd be happy to interpret any questions you might have.

References

Abelson, R. 1975. Concepts for representing mundane reality in plans. In *Representation and understanding*, edited by D. Bobrow and A. Collins. New York: Academic Press. 273–309.

Anderson, R. B. W. 1976. Perspectives on the role of an interpreter. In *Translation: Applications and research*, edited by R. Brislin. New York: Gardner Press. 208–28.

Aronsson, K. 1991. Facework and control in multiparty talk: A pediatric case study. In *Asymmetries in dialogue*, edited by I. Marková and K. Foppa. Savage, Md.: Barnes and Noble Books. 49–74.

Baker, C. 1977. Regulators and turn-taking in American Sign Language discourse. In *On the other hand: New perspectives on American Sign Language*, edited by L. Friedman. New York: Academic Press. 215–36.

Baker, C., and D. Cokely. 1980. *American Sign Language: A teacher's resource text on grammar and culture*. Silver Spring, Md.: TJ Publishers.

Baker-Shenk, C. 1991. The interpreter: machine, advocate, or ally? In *Expanding horizons: Proceedings of the 1991 RID Convention*, edited by J. Plant-Moeller. Silver Spring, Md.: RID. 120–40.

Bakhtin, M. [1975] 1986. *The dialogic imagination*. Austin: University of Texas Press.

Barik, H. 1969. A study of simultaneous interpretation. Ph.D. diss., University of North Carolina, Chapel Hill.

———. 1973. Simultaneous interpretation: Temporal and quantitative data. *Language and Speech* 16:237–70.

———. 1975. Simultaneous interpretation: Qualitative and linguistic data. *Language and Speech* 18:272–97.

Bartlett, F. C. 1932. *Remembering: A study in experimental and social psychology*. Cambridge: Cambridge University Press.

Bateson, G. 1955. A theory of play and fantasy. *American Psychological Association Psychiatric Research Reports*, vol. 2. Reprinted in Bateson, *Steps to an ecology of mind*. 177–93.

———. 1972. *Steps to an ecology of mind*. New York: Ballantine.

Becker, A. L. 1988. Language in particular: A lecture. In *Linguistics in context: Connecting observation and understanding*, edited by D. Tannen. Norwood, N.J.: Ablex. 17–35.

217

Berk-Seligson, S. 1990. *The bilingual courtroom.* Chicago: University of Chicago Press.

Bobrow, D., and D. Norman. 1975. Some principles of memory schemata. In *Representation and understanding,* edited by D. Bobrow and A. Collins. New York: Academic Press. 131–49.

Bonanno, M. 1995. Hedges in the medical intake interview: Discourse task, gender and role. Ph.D. diss., Georgetown University.

Brasel, B. 1976. The effects of fatigue on the competence of interpreters for the deaf. In *Selected readings in the integration of Deaf students at CSUN,* edited by H. Murphy. Northridge, Calif.: California State University.

Briggs. C. L. 1986. *Learning how to ask: A sociolinguistic appraisal of the role of the interview in social science research.* New York: Cambridge University Press.

Brislin, R., ed. 1976. *Translation: Applications and research.* New York: Gardner Press.

Casagrande, J. 1954. The ends of translation. *International Journal of American Linguistics* 20:335–40.

Catford, J. 1965. *A linguistic theory of translation: An essay in applied linguistics.* Oxford: Oxford University Press.

Chafe, W. 1977. Creativity in verbalization and its implications for the nature of stored knowledge. In *Discourse production and comprehension,* edited by R. Freedle. Norwood, N.J.: Ablex. 41–55.

Chernov, G. 1969. Linguistic problems in the compression of speech in simultaneous interpretation. *Tetradi Perevodchika* 6:52–65.

———. 1973. Towards a psycholinguistic model of simultaneous interpretation. *Linguistische Arbeitsberichte* 7:225–60.

Cicourel, A. 1981. Language and medicine. In *Language in the USA,* edited by C. Ferguson and S. B. Heath. New York: Cambridge University Press.

———. 1983. Hearing is not believing: Language and the structure of belief in medical communication. In *The social organization of doctor-patient communication,* edited by S. Fisher and A. Todd. Washington, D.C.: Center for Applied Linguistics.

Clayman, S. 1992. Footing in the achievement of neutrality: The case of news interview discourse. In *Talk at work: Interaction in institutional settings,* edited by P. Drew and J. Heritage. Cambridge: Cambridge University Press. 163–98.

Cokely, D. 1982. The interpreted medical interview: It loses something in the translation. *The Reflector* 3:5–1 1.

———. 1992. *Interpretation: A sociolinguistic model.* Burtonsville, Md.: Linstok Press.

Davis, J. 1989. Distinguishing language contact phenomena in ASL interpretation. In *The sociolinguistics of the Deaf community,* edited by C. Lucas. San Diego: Academic Press. 85–102.

———. 1990. Linguistic transference and interference: Interpreting between English and ASL. In *Sign language research: Theoretical issues,* edited by C. Lucas. Washington, D.C.: Gallaudet University Press. 308–21.

DiPietro, L. 1979. *Deaf patients: Special needs, special responses.* Washington, D.C.: National Academy of Gallaudet College.

Donaghy, W. 1984. *The interview: Skills and applications.* Glenview, Ill.: Scott, Foresman. 301–12.

Earwood, C. 1983. Will you please sign? *Deaf American* 36.1:15–16.

Eckert, P. 1993. Cooperative competition in adolescent "girl talk." In *Gender and conversational interaction,* edited by D. Tannen. Oxford: Oxford University Press. 32–61.

Edmondson, W. 1986. Cognition, conversing and interpreting. In *Interlingual and intercultural communication,* edited by J. House and S. Blum-Kulka. Tüibingen: Gunter Narr. 7. 129–38.

Edwards, J., and M. Lampert. 1993. *Taking data: Transcription and coding in discourse research.* Hillsdale, N.J.: Lawrence Erlbaum Associates.

Ehlich, K. 1993. HIAT: A transcription system for discourse data. In *Talking data: Transcription and coding in discourse research,* edited by J. Edwards and M. Lampert. Hillsdale, N.J.: Lawrence Erlbaum Associates. 123–48.

Englund Dimitrova, B. 1991. När tva samtalar genom en tredje. lnteraktion och icke-verbal kommunikation i medicinska möten med tolk. *Rapporter om tvakighet* 7. Stockholm: Stockholm University, Centre for Research on Bilingualism.

Filbeck, D. 1972. The passive, an unpleasant experience. *Bible Translator* 23:331–36.

Fillmore, C. 1976. The need for a frame semantics within linguistics. *Statistical Methods in Linguistics,* 5–29.

Fink, B. 1982. Being ignored can be bliss: Ho language interpreter. *Deaf American* 34.6:5–9. (Reprinted from *Disabled USA,* Fall 1981).

Firth, J. R. 1951. *Papers in Linguistics: 1934–1951.* London: Oxford University Press.

Fisher, S. 1983. Doctor talk/patient talk: How treatment decisions are negotiated in doctor-patient communication. In *The social organization of doctor-patient communication,* edited by S. Fisher and A. D. Todd. Washington, D.C.: Center for Applied Linguistics. 135–57.

Ford, J. 1976. A linguistic analysis of doctor-patient communication problems. Ph.D. diss., Georgetown University.

Frake, C. 1977. Plying frames can be dangerous: Some reflections on methodology in cognitive anthropology. *Quarterly Newsletter of the Institute for Comparative Human Development,* Rockefeller University, 1:1–7.

Frankel, R. 1984. Talking in interviews: A dispreference for patient-initiated questions in physician-patient encounters. In *Interactional competence,* edited by G. Psathas and R. Frankel. New York: Irvington.

Friedman, L. 1975. Space, time, and person reference in American Sign Language. *Language* 51:940–61.

———, ed. 1977. *On the other hand.* New York: Academic Press. 215–38.

Frishberg, N. 1990. *Interpreting: An introduction.* Silver Spring, Md.: RID.

Garfinkel, H. 1967. *Studies in ethnomethodology.* Englewood Cliffs, N.J.: Prentice-Hall.

———. 1974. On the origins of the term "ethnomethodology." In *Ethnomethodology,* edited by R. Turner. Harmondsworth: Penguin.

Gerver, D. 1969. The effects of source language presentation rate on the performance of simultaneous conference interpreters. In *Proceedings of the 2nd Louisville Conference on rate and/or frequency controlled speech*, edited by E. Foulke. University of Louisville. 162–84.

———. 1971. Simultaneous interpretation and human information processing. Ph.D. diss., Oxford University.

———. 1974a. The effects of noise on the performance of simultaneous interpreters: Accuracy of performance. *Acta Psychologica* 38:159–67.

———. 1974b. Simultaneous listening and speaking and retention of prose. *Quarterly Journal of Experimental Psychology* 26:337–42.

———. 1976. Empirical studies of simultaneous interpretation: A review and a model. In *Translation: applications and research*, edited by R. Brislin. New York: Gardner Press. 165–207.

Gile, D. 1990. Scientific research vs. personal theories in the investigation of interpretation. In *Aspects of applied and experimental research on conference interpretation*, edited by L. Gran and C. Taylor. Universitá degli Studi di Trieste: Campanotto Editore Udine. 28–41.

Goffman, E. 1974. *Frame analysis.* New York: Harper and Row.

———. 1981. *Forms of talk.* Philadelphia: University of Pennsylvania Press.

Goldman-Eisler, F. 1967. Sequential temporal patterns and cognitive processes in speech. *Language and Speech* 10:122–32.

———. 1968. *Psycholinguistics: Experiments in spontaneous speech.* London: Academic Press.

———. 1972. Segmentation of input in simultaneous interpretation. *Journal of Psycholinguistic Research* 1:127–40.

Goodwin, C. 1995. The social life of aphasia. Paper presented at GLS 1995: Developments in Discourse Analysis. Washington, D.C.: Georgetown University.

Gumperz, J. J. 1982. *Discourse strategies.* Cambridge: Cambridge University Press.

Haas, C., E. Fleetwood, and M. Ernest. 1995. An analysis of ASL variation within DeafBlind-DeafBlind interaction: Question forms, backchanneling, and turn-taking. In *Gallaudet University Communication Forum 1995*, edited by C. Lucas. Washington, D.C.: Gallaudet University School of Communication Student Forum.

Halliday, M. A. K., A. McIntosh, and P. Strevens. 1964. *The linguistic sciences and language teaching.* London: Longman.

Hamilton, H. 1994. *Conversations with an Alzheimer's patient: An interactional sociolinguistic study.* Cambridge: Cambridge University Press.

Harris, B. 1990. Norms in interpretation. *Target* 2.1:115–19.

Hatim, B., and I. Mason. 1990. *Discourse and the translator.* London: Longman.

Head, Sir H. 1920. *Studies in neurology.* Oxford: Oxford University Press.

Herbert, J. 1968. *The interpreter's handbook: How to become a conference interpreter.* Geneva: Georg and Cie, S.A.

Hohenberg, J. 1983. *The professional journalist.* New York: Holt, Rinehart, and Winston.

Hoyle, S. 1993. Participation frameworks in sportscasting play: Imaginary and literal footings. In *Framing in discourse*, edited by D. Tannen. Oxford: Oxford University Press. 114–45.

Hromosová, A. 1972. A study of memory in interpreting. *Acta Universitatis* 17.

Hymes, D. 1972. Models of the interaction of language and social life. In *Directions in sociolinguistics: The ethnography of communication*, edited by J. Gumperz and D. Hymes. New York: Holt, Rinehart, and Winston. 35–71.

Jakobson, R. 1959. On linguistic aspects of translation. In *On translation*, edited by R. Brower. Cambridge: Harvard University Press. 232–39.

Johnson, R. E., and C. Erting. 1989. Ethnicity and socialization in a classroom for Deaf children. In *The sociolinguistics of the Deaf community*, edited by C. Lucas. San Diego: Academic Press. 41–84.

Johnson, R. E., S. K. Liddell, and C. Erting. 1989. Unlocking the curriculum: Principles for achieving access in Deaf education. Washington, D.C.: Gallaudet Research Institute Occasional Paper, 89–3.

Kade, O. 1968. Kommunikationswissenschaftliche: Probleme der ubersetzung. In *Grundfragen der Ubersetzungswissenschaft.- Beihefte sur Zeitschrfit Fremdsprachen*, edited by A. Neubert. Vol. 2, 3–20.

Kade, O., and C. Cartellieri. 1971. Some methodological aspects of simultaneous interpretation. *Babel* 17:12–16.

Kaufert, J., and W. Koolage. 1984. Role conflict among culture broilers: The experience of native Canadian medical interpreters. *Social Science Medicine* 18.3:283–86.

Kaufert, J., P. Leyland, J. O'Neil, and W. Koolage. 1985. Advocacy, media, and native medical interpreters. In *Advocacy and anthropology*, edited by R. Paine. St. Johns, Newfoundland: Institute of Social and Economic Research Memorial, University of Newfoundland.

Keith, H. 1984. Liaison interpreting—an exercise in linguistic interaction. In *Translation theory and its implementation in the teaching of translating and interpreting*, edited by W. Wilss and G. Thome. Tübingen: Gunter Narr Verlag. 308–17.

Kibrik, A. E. 1977. *The methodology of field investigations in linguistics.* Janua Linguarum, Series Minor. The Hague: Mouton.

Knapp-Potthoff, A., and K. Knapp. 1986. Interweaving two discourses—The difficult task of the non-professional interpreter. In *Interlingual and intercultural communication*, edited by J. House and S. Blum-Kulka. Tübingen: Gunter Narr Verlag. 151–68.

———. 1987. The man (or woman) in the middle: Discoursal aspects of non-professional interpreting. In *Analyzing intercultural communication*, edited by K. Knapp, W. Enninger, and A. Knapp-Potthoff. Berlin: Mouton de Gruyter.

Kochman, T. 1986. Strategic ambiguity in Black speech genres: Cross-cultural interference in participant-observation research. *Text* 6.2:153–70.

Kuipers, B. 1975. A frame for frames. In *Representation and understanding*, edited by D. Bobrow and A. Collins. New York: Academic Press. 151–84.

Kulick, D. 1982. Interpretation and discourse. In *Om Tolkning, Praktisk Lingvistik* 7. Lund: Institutionen för lingvistik, Lunds universitet. 5–45.

Labov, W. 1972a. Some principles of linguistic methodology. *Language in Society* 1:97–120.

———. 1972b. *Sociolinguistic patterns.* Philadelphia: Pennsylvania University Press.

———. 1984. Field methods of the project on linguistic change and variation. In *Language in use,* edited by J. Baugh and J. Sherzer. Englewood Cliffs, N.J.: Prentice-Hall.

Landsberg, M. 1976. Translation theory: An appraisal of some general problems. *Meta* 21:235–51.

Lang, R. 1976. Interpreters in local courts in Papua New Guinea. In *Language and politics,* edited by W. M. O'Barr and J. F. O'Barr. The Hague-Paris: Mouton.

———. 1978. Behavioral aspects of liaison interpreters in Papua New Guinea: Some preliminary observations. In *Language interpretation and communication,* edited by D. Gerver and H. W. Sinaico. New York: Plenum. 231–44.

Larson, M. 1984. *Meaning-based translation: A guide to cross-language equivalence.* Lanham, Md.: University Press of America.

Lefevre, A. 1992. *Translation/history/culture: A sourcebook.* London: Routledge.

Levinson, S. 1983. *Pragmatics.* Cambridge: Cambridge University Press.

Liddell, S., and M. Metzger. 1995. Alternate physical contexts: Comprehensibility in an American Sign Language narrative. Unpublished manuscript.

Llewellyn-Jones, P. 1981. Simultaneous interpreting. In *Perspectives on British Sign Language and deafness,* edited by B. Woll, J. Kyle, and M. Deuchar. London: Croom Helm. 89–104.

Locker McKee, R. 1992. Footing shifts in American Sign Language lectures. Ph.D. diss., University of California, Los Angeles.

Lucas, C. 1994. The importance of interviewer characteristics. Paper presented at NWAVE 23. Stanford University.

Lucas, C., and C. Valli. 1989. Language contact in the American Deaf community. In *The sociolinguistics of the Deaf community,* edited by C. Lucas. San Diego: Academic Press. 11–40.

———. 1990. ASL, English, and contact signing. In *Sign language research: Theoretical issues,* edited by C. Lucas. Washington, D.C.: Gallaudet University Press. 288–307.

———. 1991. ASL or contact signing: Issues of judgment. *Language in Society* 20:201–16.

———. 1992. *Language contact in the American Deaf community.* San Diego: Academic Press.

MacKinnon, R., and R. Michels. 1971. *The psychiatric interview in clinical practice.* Philadelphia: W. B. Saunders Co.

Mason, I. 1990. The interpreter as listener: An observation of response in the oral mode of translating. In *Reception and response-hearer creativity and the analysis of spoken and written texts,* edited by G. McGregor and R. S. White. London: Routledge. 145–59.

Mather, Susan. 1994. Adult/Deaf-toddler discourse. In *Post Milan–ASL and English literacy: Issues, trends, and research,* edited by B. Snider. Washington, D.C.: Gallaudet University College for Continuing Education. 283–97.

McDowell, E. 1986. Information-gathering interviewing in the technical writer's world of work. *Technical Communication* 33:49–50.

McIntire, M., and G. Sanderson. 1995. Who's in charge here?: Perceptions of empowerment and role in the interpreting setting. *Journal of Interpretation* 7.1:99–113.

Mehta, V. 1971. A second voice. In *John is easy to please*. New York: Farrar, Straus, and Giroux. 3–25.

Meier, R. 1990. Person deixis in American Sign Language. In *Theoretical issues in sign language research*. Vol. 1. *Linguistics*, edited by S. Fischer and P. Siple. Chicago: University of Chicago Press.

Merritt, M. 1976. On questions following questions (in service encounters). *Language in Society* 5.3:315–57.

Metzger, M. 1995. Constructed dialogue and constructed action in American Sign Language. In *Sociolinguistics in Deaf communities*, edited by C. Lucas. Washington, D.C.: Gallaudet University Press. 255–71.

Miller, J. G. 1964. Adjusting to overloads of information. *Research on Public Assistance for Nervous and Mental Disease* 42:87–100.

Minsky, M. 1975. A framework for representing knowledge. In *The psychology of computer vision*, edited by P. Winston. New York: McGraw Hill. 211–77.

Mishler, E. 1984. *The discourse of medicine: Dialects of medical interviews*. Norwood, N.J.: Ablex.

———. 1986. *Research interviewing: Context and narrative*. Cambridge: Harvard University Press.

———. 1991. Representing discourse: The rhetoric of transcription. *Journal of Narrative and Life History* 1.4:255–80.

Moser, B. 1978. Simultaneous interpretation: A hypothetical model and its practical application. In *Language interpretation and communication*, edited by D. Gerver and H. Sinalko. New York: Plenum Press. 353–68.

Müller, F. 1989. Translation in bilingual conversation: Pragmatic aspects of translators interaction. *Journal of Pragmatics* 13:713–39.

Neubert, A. 1968. Pragmatische aspekete der Übersetzung. In *Grundfragen der Übersetzungswissenschaft*, edited by A. Neubert. Behhefte sur Zeitschrift Fremdsprachen. 21–33.

Newmark, P. 1974. Further propositions on translation, Part 2. *The Incorporated Linguist*. 13. 62–71.

———. 1981. *Approaches to translation*. Elmsford, N.Y.: Pergamon Press.

Nida, E. 1964. *Toward a science of translating with special reference to principles and procedures involved in Bible translating*. Leiden: E. J. Brill.

———. 1975. Componential analysis of meaning. In *Approaches to semantics*, edited by T. Sebeok. The Hague: Mouton.

———. 1976. A framework for the analysis and the evaluation of theories of translation. In *Translation: Applications and research*, edited by R. Brislin. New York: Gardner Press. 47–91.

Nida, E., and C. Taber. 1969. *The theory and practice of translation*. Leiden: E. J. Brill.

Ochs, E. 1979. Transcription as theory. In *Developmental pragmatics*, edited by E. Ochs and B. Schieffelin. New York: Academic Press. 43–72.

Oléron, P., and H. Nanpon. 1965. Recherches sur la traduction simultanée. *Journal de Psychologie Normale et Pathologique* 45:483–98.

Paneth, E. 1957. An investigation into conference interpreting. Master's thesis. London University.

Parsons, T. 1964. Professions. *International Encyklopedia of the Social Sciences.* Vol. 12.

Pergnier, M. 1978. Language meaning and message meaning: Towards a sociolinguistic approach to translation. In *Language interpretation and communication,* edited by D. Gerver and H. Sinaiko. New York: Plenum Press. 199–204.

Pintner, I. 1969. Der einfluss der übung und konzentration auf simultanes sprechen und horen. Doctoral thesis. University of Vienna.

Prince, C. 1986. Hablado con el doctor: Communication problems between doctors and their Spanish-speaking patients. Ph.D. diss., Stanford University: University Microfilms International.

Prince, E. 1981. Towards a taxonomy of given-new information. In *Radical pragmatics,* edited by P. Cole. New York: Academic Press. 223–56.

Prince, E., J. Frader, and C. Bosk. 1982. On hedging in physician-physician discourse. In *Linguistics and the professions,* edited by R. DiPietro. New Jersey: Ablex Publishing Corporation. 83–97.

Ramler, S. 1988. Origins and challenges of simultaneous interpretation: The Nuremburg Trials experience. *Proceedings of the Twenty-ninth Annual Conference of the American Translators Assocation.* 437–40.

Ray, L. 1976. Multidimensional translation: Poetry. In *Translation: applications and research,* edited by R. Brislin. New York: Gardner Press. 261–78.

Ribeiro, B. 1993. Framing in psychotic discourse. In *Framing in discourse,* edited by D. Tannen. Oxford: Oxford University Press. 77–113.

Richards, I. 1953. Toward a theory of translating. *American Anthropological Association, Studies in Chinese Thought* 55:247–62.

Roberts, R. 1987. Spoken language interpreting vs. sign language interpreting. *Proceedings of the 28th Annual Conference of the American Translators Association.* 293–306.

Rosenfeld, E. 1996. Participant structures in therapeutic discourse: An analysis of dyadic discourse in marital therapy. Ph.D. diss., Georgetown University.

Roy, C. 1986. Who is a native speaker? *Journal of Interpretation* 3:63–66.

———. 1989a. A sociolinguistic analysis of the interpreter's role in the turn exchanges of an interpreted event. Ph.D. diss., Washington, D.C.: Georgetown University.

———. 1989b. Features of discourse in an American Sign Language lecture. In *Sociolinguistics of the Deaf community,* edited by C. Lucas. San Diego: Academic Press. 231–51.

———. 1993. A sociolinguistic analysis of the interpreter's role in simultaneous talk in interpreted interaction. *Multilingua* 12.4:341–63.

Sacks, H., E. Schegloff, and G. Jefferson. 1974. A simplest systematics for the organization of turn-taking in conversation. *Language* 50.4:696–735.

———. 1978. A simplest systematics for the organization of turn-taking in conversation. In *Studies in the organization of conversational interaction,* edited by J. Schenlein. New York: Academic Press. 7–55.

Savory, T. 1968. *The art of translation.* Boston: The Writer.

Schank, R., and R. Abelson. 1977. *Scripts, plans, goals, and understanding: An inquiry into human knowledge structures.* Hillsdale, N.J.: Erlbaum.

Schegloff, E. 1972. Sequencing in conversational openings. In *Directions in sociolinguistics,* edited by J. Gumperz and D. Hymes. New York: Holt, Rinehart, and Winston. 346–80.

Schegloff, E., and Harvey Sacks. 1973. Opening up closings. *Semiotica* 7.4:289–327.

Schegloff, E., G. Jefferson, and H. Sacks. 1977. The preference for self-correction in the organization of repair in conversation. *Language* 53:361–82.

Schiffrin, D. 1987. *Discourse markers.* Cambridge: Cambridge University Press.

———. 1993. "Speaking for another" in sociolinguistic interviews. In *Framing in discourse,* edited by D. Tannen. New York: Oxford University Press. 231–63.

———. 1994. *Approaches to discourse.* Oxford: Blackwell.

Seleskovitch, D. 1965. Colloque sur l'enseignement de l'interpretation. Paris: Association Internationale des Interpretes de Conference.

———. 1977. Why interpretation is not tantamount to translating languages. *The Incorporated Linguist* 16.2:27–33.

———. 1978. *Interpreting for international conferences.* Washington, D.C.: Pen and Booth.

Shuy, R. 1972. Sociolinguistics and the medical history. Paper presented at the Third International Conference of Applied Linguistics.

———. 1976. The medical interview: Problems in communication. *Primary Care* 3.3:375–86.

———. 1979. Language policy in medicine: Some emerging issues. In *Language in public life,* edited by J. Alatis and G. Tucker. Washington, D.C.: Georgetown University Press.

———. 1983. Three types of interference to an effective exchange of information in the medical interview. In *The social organization of doctor-patient communication,* edited by S. Fisher and A. Todd. Washington, D.C.: Center for Applied Linguistics. 189–202.

———. 1987. A sociolinguistic view of interpreter education. In *New dimensions in interpreter education: Curriculum and instruction,* edited by M. McIntire. Proceedings from the Sixth National Conference of Interpreter Trainers. Silver Spring, Md.: RID Publications.

———. 1990. A brief history of American sociolinguistics 1949–1989. *Historiographia Linguistica* 17:1/2. 183–209.

———. 1995. Getting people to admit their guilt: A tacit theory of language. Paper presented at GLS: Developments in Discourse Analysis. Washington, D.C.: Georgetown University. February 17–19, 1995.

Shuy, R., W. Wolfram, and W. K. Riley. 1968. *Field techniques in an urban language study.* Washington, D.C.: Center for Applied Linguistics.

Siple, L. 1995. The use of addition in sign language transliteration. Ph.D. diss., University of New York–Buffalo.

Skopek, L. 1975. Sociolinguistic aspects of the medical interview. Ph.D. diss., Georgetown University.

Smith, F. 1993. The pulpit and woman's place: Gender and the framing of the "exegetical self" in sermon performances. In *Framing in discourse*, edited by D. Tannen. Oxford: Oxford University Press. 146–75.

Softkey International. 1994. *American Heritage electronic dictionary*. Boston: Houghton Mifflin Company.

Solow, S. N. 1981. *Sign language interpreting: A basic resource book*. Silver Spring, Md.: National Association of the Deaf.

Straehle, C. 1993. "Samuel?" "Yes, Dear": Teasing and conversational rapport. In *Framing in discourse*, edited by D. Tannen. Oxford: Oxford University Press. 210–30.

Supalla, S. 1986. Manually Coded English: The modality question in signed language development. Master's thesis, University of Illinois, Urbana-Champaign.

———. 1991. Manually Coded English: The modality question in signed language development. In *Theoretical issues in sign language research*, vol. 2, *Psychology*, edited by P. Siple and S. Fischer. Chicago: University of Chicago Press. 85–109.

Tannen, D. 1979. What's in a frame? Surface evidence for underlying expectations. In *New directions in discourse processing*, edited by R. Freedle. Norwood, N.J.: Ablex. 137–81.

———. 1984. *Conversational style: Analyzing talk among friends*. Norwood, N.J.: Ablex.

———. 1986. *That's not what I meant*. New York: Ballantine Books.

———. 1989. *Talking voices: Repetition. dialogue, and imagery in conversational discourse*. Cambridge: Cambridge University Press.

———. 1993. Interactional sociolinguistics. *Oxford Encyclopedia of Language*. Oxford: Oxford University Press. 9–12.

———, ed. 1993. *Framing in discourse*. Oxford: Oxford University Press.

Tannen, D., and C. Wallat. 1982. A sociolinguistic analysis of multiple demands on the pediatrician in doctor/mother/patient interaction. In *Linguistics and the professions*, edited by R. Di Pietro. Norwood, N.J.: Ablex. 39–50.

———. 1983. Doctor/mother/child communication: Linguistic analysis of pediatric interaction. In *The social organization of doctor-patient communication*, edited by S. Fisher and A. D. Todd. Washington, D.C.: Center for Applied Linguistics. 203–19.

———. 1987. Interactive frames and knowledge schemas in interaction: Examples from a medical examination/interview. *Social Psychology Quarterly* 50.2:205–16. (Reprinted in *Framing in discourse*, edited by D. Tannen. New York: Oxford University Press, 1993. 57–76.)

———. 1993. Interactive frames and knowledge schemas in interaction: Examples from a medical examination/interview. In *Framing in discourse*, edited by D. Tannen. New York: Oxford University Press. 57–76.

Thieberger, R. 1972. Le language de la traduction. In *La Traduction*, edited by J. Ladmiral. Paris: Didier and Larousse. 75–84.

Treisman, A. 1965. The effects of redundancy and familiarity on translating and repeating back a foreign and a native language. *British Journal of Psychology* 56: 369–79.

Van Dam, I. M. 1989. Strategies of simultaneous interpretation. In *The theoretical and practical aspects of teaching conference interpretation,* edited by L. Gran and J. Dodds. Udine: Campanotto Editore. 167–76.

Van Hoof, H. 1962. *Théorie et pratique de la traduction.* Munich: Max Hueber.

Vinay, J., and J. Darbelnet. 1958. *Stylistique comparée du français et de l'anglais: Méthode de traduction.* Paris: Didier.

Voloshinov, V. [1929] 1986. *Marxism and the philosophy of language,* translated by L. Matejka and I. Titunik. Cambridge: Harvard University Press.

Wadensjö, C. 1992. *Interpreting as interaction: On dialogue-interpreting in immigration hearings and medical encounters.* Linköping University: Linköping Studies in Arts and Science.

Watanabe, S. 1993. Cultural differences in framing: American and Japanese group discussions. In *Framing in discourse,* edited by D. Tannen. Oxford: Oxford University Press. 176–209.

Welford, A. 1968. *The fundamentals of skill.* London: Methuen.

West, C. 1983. "Ask me no questions . . ." An analysis of queries and replies in physician-patient dialogues. In *The social organization of doctor-patient communication,* edited by S. Fisher and A. Todd. Washington, D.C.: Center for Applied Linguistics. 75–106.

Wilss, W. 1977. *Ubersetzungswissenschaft: Probleme und methoden.* Stuttgart: Klett.

———. 1982. *The science of translation: Problems and methods.* Tübigen: Gunter Narr Verlag.

Winston, E. 1989. Transliteration: What's the message. In *The sociolinguistics of the Deaf community,* edited by C. Lucas. San Diego: Academic Press. 147–64.

———. 1991. Spatial referencing and cohesion in an American Sign Language text. *Sign Language Studies* 73:397–410.

———. 1992. Space and involvement in an American Sign Language lecture. In *Expanding horizons: Proceedings of the twelfth national convention of the Registry of Interpreters for the Deaf,* edited by J. Plant-Moeller. Silver Spring, Md.: RID. 93–105.

———. 1993. Spatial mapping in comparative discourse frames in an American Sign Language lecture. Ph.D. diss., Georgetown University.

Winston, E., and C. Ball. 1994. Towards a corpus of ASL. Paper presented at NWAVE 23. Stanford University.

Witter-Merithew, A. 1986. Claiming our destiny. In *RID Views* (October): 12.

Wolff, K., ed. and trans. 1964. *The sociology of Georg Simmel (1885–1918).* New York: Free Press.

Wolfson, N. 1979. The conversational historical present alternation. *Language* 55:168–82.

Zimmer, J. 1989. ASL/English interpreting in an interactive setting. In *Proceedings of the 30th Annual Conference of the American Translators Assocation,* edited by D. Hammond. Medford, N.J.: Learned Information. 225–31.

Index